Vietnam

The Ultimate Vietnam Travel Guide By A Traveler For A Traveler

The Best Travel Tips: Where To Go, What To See And Much More

SECOND EDITION

© Copyright 2016 by Seven Tree Group Inc. - All rights reserved.

This document is geared towards providing exact and reliable information in regards to the topic and issue covered. The publication is sold with the idea that the publisher is not required to render accounting, officially permitted, or otherwise, qualified services. If advice is necessary, legal or professional, a practiced individual in the profession should be ordered.

- From a Declaration of Principles which was accepted and approved equally by a Committee of the American Bar Association and a Committee of Publishers and Associations.

In no way is it legal to reproduce, duplicate, or transmit any part of this document in either electronic means or in printed format. Recording of this publication is strictly prohibited and any storage of this document is not allowed unless with written permission from the publisher. All rights reserved.

The information provided herein is stated to be truthful and consistent, in that any liability, in terms of inattention or otherwise, by any usage or abuse of any policies, processes, or directions contained within is the solitary and utter responsibility of the recipient reader. Under no circumstances will any legal responsibility or blame be held against the publisher for any reparation, damages, or monetary loss due to the information herein, either directly or indirectly.

Respective authors own all copyrights not held by the publisher.

The information herein is offered for informational purposes solely, and is universal as so. The presentation of the information is without contract or any type of guarantee assurance.

The trademarks that are used are without any consent, and the publication of the trademark is without permission or backing by the trademark owner. All trademarks and brands within this book are for clarifying purposes only and are the owned by the owners themselves, not affiliated with this document.

Table of Contents

VIETNAM

WHY LOST TRAVELERS GUIDES?

CHAPTER 1 - BRIEF HISTORY OF VIETNAM

CHAPTER 2 - GEOGRAPHY AND CLIMATE

CHAPTER 3 - CULTURE AND RELIGION

CHAPTER 4 - VISA AND IMMIGRATION

CHAPTER 5 - GETTING TO VIETNAM

CHAPTER 6 - GETTING AROUND

CHAPTER 7 - ACCOMMODATION

CHAPTER 8 - FESTIVALS AND CULTURAL EVENTS

CHAPTER 9 - SURVIVAL GUIDE AND SAFETY TIPS

CHAPTER 10 - TRAVEL ESSENTIALS

CHAPTER 11 - HO CHI MINH CITY

CHAPTER 12 - HANOI

CHAPTER 13 – THE MEKONG DELTA

CHAPTER 14 – HOI AN

CHAPTER 15 – HA LONG BAY

CONCLUSION

Why Lost Travelers Guides?

First, we want to wish you an amazing time in Vietnam when you plan to visit. Also we would like to thank you and congratulate you for downloading our travel guide, *"Vietnam; The Ultimate Vietnam Travel Guide By A Traveler For A Traveler".*

Allow us to explain our beginnings, and the reason we created Lost Travelers. Lost Travelers was created due to one simple problem that other guides on the market did not solve; loss of time. Considering it's the 21st century and everything is available online, why do we still purchase guidebooks? To save us time! That's right.

Since the goal is to be efficient and save time, we did not understand why there are several guidebooks on the market that are of 500 to 1000 page' long. We do not believe one needs that much bluff to get an overview of the location and some remarkable suggestions. Considering many guidebooks on the market are filled with "suggestions" that were sponsored for, we have decided to take a different approach and provide our travelers with an honest opinion and decline any sort of sponsorship. This simply allows us to cut off any nonsense and create our guides the Lost Travelers style.

Our mission is simple; to create an easy to follow guide book that outlines the best of activities to do in our limited time at the destination. This easily saves you your most valuable asset; your time. You no longer need to spend hours looking through a massive book, or spend hours searching for information on the internet as we have completed the whole process for you. The best part is we provide you our e-guides for one third the price of the leading brand, and our paper copy for only half the price.

Thanks again for choosing us, we hope you enjoy!

Section 1
General Guide

Chapter 1 - Brief History of Vietnam

Modern-day Vietnamese trace their ancestry to the Lac people who founded a Bronze Age civilization in the first millennium BC near the fertile Red River Delta in the north. In the third century BC, a Chinese military adventurer conquered the Vietnamese kingdom of Van Lang and incorporated the Red River Delta into his expanding realm in Southern China. China eventually integrated Vietnam into its Chinese empire a hundred years later.

The more than 1,000 years of Chinese rule wrought significant changes in Vietnam's culture and society as its people were introduced to Chinese art, literature, architecture, language, ideas, religion, political system and social institutions. Ethnic Vietnamese were torn between their attraction to Chinese culture and their desire to resist the colonist's political grip. In AD 939, however, Vietnamese rebels took advantage of China's political chaos and restored national independence.

The Vietnamese Empire known as Dai Viet flourished, expanded steadily southward, and gradually formed its own institutions over a period of several hundred years. China periodically made attempts to regain control of Vietnam, but they were repulsed under the dynasty of the Ly (1000-1225AD) and the Tran (1225-1400AD). The expansion to the south continued at the expense of Champa, their southern neighbor and a civilization that flourished in South Vietnam during China's domination of the north. The Indian-influenced Champa kingdom was founded and ruled by non-Vietnamese people, the Chams.

Chinese rule was restored in the early 15th century, but a national revolt led by the Le Loi cut the reign short. This led to the formation of the Le Dynasty, which lasted from 1428 to 1788. By the 17th century, the Le Dynasty gained complete control of Southern Vietnam and ruled over the entire Mekong River Delta. The Le leadership, however, would later slip into a civil strife between two warring royal families, the Trinh in northern Vietnam and the Nguyen in the south. The political turmoil happened at a time when European explorers were just starting to extend their missionary and commercial activities in the East, including Southeast Asia.

A peasant uprising led by the Tay Son brothers overthrew the Nguyen and the Trinh in 1771 and united the country under the leadership of the most competent among the Tay Son brothers, Emperor Nguyen Hue. His reign was short, however, as his kingdom was subdued by a military force organized by a Nguyen prince with the help of a French missionary bishop. The victory ushered in the Nguyen Dynasty (1802-1945) and reunified the country under the leadership of Emperor Gia Long. The alliance between France and the Nguyen dynasty, however, soon turned sour as both Gia Long and his son and successor, Minh Mang, refused to grant missionary and commercial privileges to France.

The French government used the execution and harassment of Catholic missionaries by the Vietnamese emperors as a pretext for their invasion and colonization of Vietnam. In September 1858, the French force aided by Spanish troops attacked southern provinces near Saigon and conquered the territory, which became known as the French colony of Conchinchina. France completed its conquest of Vietnam in 1884 when it established a protectorate over Northern and Central Vietnam. They set their capital in Saigon. In 1895, Vietnam was integrated into a French-ruled Indochinese Union along with the protectorates of Cambodia and Laos. Over the next decades, the French protected their colonies against the attack of the Chinese who still considered Vietnam as their territory.

In 1940, Japan invaded the Indochina as part of their "Asia for Asians" campaign. Japan's revolutionary idea raised consciousness among Southeast Asian people of the fact that small and distant countries from Europe have managed to control their larger and more populous territories.

On May 19, 1941, the Viet Minh or the League for the Independence of Vietnam was set up by Ho Chi Minh at Pác Bó and seized north and central Vietnam immediately afterwards. They fought Japanese invasion with the support of China and the United States. In December 1946, the war between the Communist-led north and the French-controlled south started. The French withdrew from Vietnam in 1954 and left a divided nation.

In the 1960s, the United States sent troops, ammunition and support to its Vietnamese allies in the south to fight the communists in what is variably known as the Vietnam War, the American War, or the Second Indochina War. On the other hand, the Viet Cong and the Communist party were fighting to reunite North and South Vietnam under communist rule.

The United States withdrew its participation in the Vietnam War in 1975 and Saigon fell to the Communists on April 30, 1975, marking the start of Vietnam's reunification.

Vietnam has since instituted sweeping economic and political reforms that led to its renaissance. A high sense of optimism pervades the resilient nation as its entrepreneurial spirit is ignited by a free market economy and the openness that allowed international visitors to bask in the richness of the country's culture and history.

Chapter 2 - Geography and Climate

Vietnam is a tropical country with a central tropical rainforest. It shares borders with China on the north and with Laos and Cambodia on the west. The South China Sea and the Pacific Ocean lie on its eastern and southern sections. The S-shaped country measures about 128,000 square miles and spans the eastern side of the Indochina Peninsula.

Vietnam is a lush tapestry of fertile deltas, winding rivers, lofty mountains, tropical lowlands, pristine forests, intriguing rock formations and caves, spectacular beaches, and breathtaking waterfalls. Its primordial jungles are home to exotic animals.

Central Vietnam is known for its natural ponds, dunes and dazzling beaches. Its high plateaus have irregular forms and elevations and are rich in volcanic soil. The ancient imperial city of Hue can be found in this region. The northern part is the location of the historic Hanoi, Red River Delta, Halong Bay, Cao Bang and Vinh Yen plains, and alpine peaks. It is home to a diverse mix of ethno-linguistic minorities. The modern Ho Chi Minh City and the Mekong River delta are located in the Southern part of Vietnam.

The main rivers in Vietnam are the Red River and the Mekong River. The principal rivers traversing Vietnam are the Ca, Han, Ma, Thach Han, and Thu Bon on the center, the Red and Thai Binh in the north, and the Dong Nai and Mekong in the South.

The Red River, also known as Song Hong, is 1,200 km long. The Lo River and the Clear River are the two main contributors to its high water volume, which frequently causes frequent flooding specially during rainy seasons. An extensive network of canals and dikes help control the Red River and route excess water to the rice-planted delta.

The Mekong River is about 4,220 kilometers long and is listed among the great rivers of the world. It originates from the Tibetan plateau and flows through the Yunnan and Tibet sections of China, divides into two separate paths below Phnom Penh, goes on to Cambodia, flows through the Mekong basin, and drains into the South China Sea. It forms the boundary between Burma and Laos and between Thailand and Laos.

Although it is entirely located in the tropics, Vietnam has varying climate and temperatures as a result of the diversity in the altitude, latitude and weather patterns. Variations in rainfall mark seasonal changes in the country's different regions.

Northern Vietnam experiences a cold humid winter in the months of November to March while the rest of the year is marked by a warm yet rainy summer. The rainy season lasts from April to October. Temperature fluctuates significantly in the Red River Delta areas on a daily basis dropping to as low as 5°c during the dry season and reaching an average of 30°c during the rainy season in the Hanoi region. Average summer temperature is 5°c. Typhoons occasionally hit the country during the summer months.

Southern Vietnam share the South's' tropical, generally warmer weather. The southwest monsoon brings heavy rains and hot, humid weather from April to September. June and July are marked by rough seas, poor weather and some flooding.

The Truong Son mountain range protects the coastline of Central Vietnam from the heavy rains brought by the southwest monsoon from April to September; hence, it is less wet than other parts of Vietnam. The situation is reversed, however, between September and December when it receives heavy rains brought by the northeast monsoon. Severe storms often hit the coast from August to November causing flood, crop damage and loss of lives.

Chapter 3 - Culture and Religion

Vietnam's constitution guarantees religious freedom but since the country's reunification in 1975, the government placed restrictions on religious activities, requiring registration and approval for all religious groups who want to operate in the country. The government exercises control over the operations of churches by requiring approval for all religious activities.

The dominant religion in Vietnam is Buddhism with nominal members comprising about 50% of the population. Many believers, however, follow a mixture of what is known as Vietnam's Triple Religion, namely, Taoism, Confucianism, and Mahayana Buddhism. Many Vietnamese are also into the practice of spirit worship.

Roman Catholic missionaries sponsored by French, Spanish and Portuguese governments introduced Christianity in the 17th century but its propagation was strictly prohibited by the imperial court. French priests were actively involved in provoking the French government to conquer Vietnam. It was under the French rule that Christianity thrived in Vietnam.

By the time independence was restored in 1954, more than two million of the population were practicing Catholics. The number has swelled to about seven million as the 20th century drew to a close. Today, an estimated 9-10% of the population are Roman Catholics. Protestants have also increased their membership. Muslims, Hindus and the Baha'i Faith make up the small minority.

The Cao Dai and Hoa Hao are millenarian religious sects that have gained popularity among the peasants and residents of the Mekong Delta. The Cao Dai has about four million members while the Hoa Hao is estimated to have 1.3 million members.

Chapter 4 - Visa and Immigration

Foreign nationals must secure a visa before entering Vietnam. Exceptions are granted to citizens of Denmark, Sweden, Finland, Norway, South Korea and Japan who do not need a visa if their intended stay will not exceed fifteen days, provided that they are holding a return ticket and their passports are valid for at least three months following entry date. Citizens of ASEAN member countries like Singapore, Malaysia and Thailand are also exempt from the Visa requirement if their intended stay will not exceed thirty days.

In general, tourist visas are for a single entry with a validity of 30 days but multiple entry visas for longer visits are also available.

Most visitors secure a Vietnamese visa in their own country prior to travelling. Processing time is around one week but many embassies will expedite the process at an additional fee.

Student visas with one-year validity are easier to obtain for those who enroll in courses at a university in Vietnam. Tourist visa holders may secure a student visa while in Vietnam but they are required to leave the country and reenter to secure the student visa stamp.

Business visas can be issued for multiple entry and have a validity of one month and more. Visa applicants, however, will need a sponsor in Vietnam to underwrite the application.

Overstaying foreign citizens face fines ranging from $10 to $50 depending on the number of days that lapsed from the expiration date of the visa and on the immigration officer's assessment.

A tourist visa holder may apply for a 30-day visa extension in Ho Chi Minh City, Hanoi, Da Nang, Hoi An, Nha Trang, and Hué through a tour agent. A second or third extension may be granted in Ho Chi Minh City and Hanoi. The first one-month extension usually cost $25 with 3-5 days processing time.

Business visa holders may apply for extension through the office that facilitated their original visa. All applications for extension should be sufficiently justified.

Chapter 5 - Getting to Vietnam

After opening its doors to international tourism and business, Vietnam has become a popular destination for travellers all over the world. Numerous flight connections and land crossing options make it easier for tourists to visit and experience its distinctive charm.

Vietnam has three major international airports but the busiest are the Tan Son Nhat Airport in Ho Chi Minh City and the No Bai Airport in Hanoi. The Da Nang Airport accommodates fewer international flights. More than a dozen domestic airports are in operation around the country.

Airlines

Vietnam's national carrier, Vietnam Airlines (vietnamairlines.com), has an extensive domestic network and an expanding international connection. Jetstar (jetstar.com), the other domestic carrier, has a more limited local operation. While options for direct flights to Vietnam have increased in recent years, a large number of visitors take indirect flights through Singapore, Hong Kong, Bangkok, or Kuala Lumpur usually at no added cost. Great value regional deals can be had with budget airlines like Jetstar (jetstar.com), Tiger Airways (tigerairways.com), and Air Asia (airasia.com), making it more attractive to combine a trip to Vietnam with other Southeast Asian countries. Travellers coming from farther places like North America or Europe can take long-haul flight to Singapore or Bangkok and proceed to Vietnam with a budget airline for a more cost-effective travel.

Airfares vary with the season with the peak months being the weeks around the Tet Festival (January to February), during Christmas and New Year Holidays, and July to August.

Airfares are at the lowest from January to June and September to the middle of December.

International carriers offering flights to Vietnam include the following:

Airlines	Destination
Aeroflot	Hanoi
Air Asia	Hanoi (from Kuala Lumpur and Bangkok)
China Southern	Hanoi
Lao Airlines	Hanoi
Vladivostok Air	Hanoi
Air China	HCMC
ANA	HCMC
Asiana	HCMC
Bangkok Airways	HCMC
China Eastern	HCMC
Jetstar	HCMC (from Singapore)
Philippine Airlines	HCMC
Qantas	HCMC
Qatar Airlines	HCMC
Royal Brunei Airlines	HCMC
Air France	Hanoi, HCMC
Cathay Pacific	Hanoi, HCMC
China Airlines	Hanoi, HCMC
EVA Air	Hanoi, HCMC
Hong Kong Airlines	Hanoi, HCMC
JAL	Hanoi, HCMC
Korean Air	Hanoi, HCMC
Lufthansa	Hanoi, HCMC
Malaysia Airlines	Hanoi, HCMC
Singapore Airlines	Hanoi, HCMC
Tiger Airways	Hanoi, HCMC (from Singapore)
United	Hanoi, HCMC
Silk Air	Hanoi, HCMC, Da Nang
THAI	Hanoi, HCMC, Da Nang

You'll likely get a good rate if you shop online but traditional flight agents can, at other times, provide better deals specifically those who buy bulk tickets at great discount from airlines.

From the airport, if travelling on your own, you can hire a taxi to take you to your preferred destination. It's probably pricier, but many hotels provide private car service from the airport to the venue. If you have not booked your stay in advance, you can request a tourist booth staff to call for room reservation.

Land Crossings

Train

China and Vietnam have two border gates but the busiest crossing is the Dong Dang, which connects Lang Son and Pingxang China. The Dong Dang international gate can be reached by train and it is only about 160 kilometers from Hanoi. If you're coming from China, you can take the train that runs from Beijing and continues to Hanoi. To enter Vietnam from China, you have to submit to an immigration process in a building located in the border gate on the Chinese side.

From the Dong Dang crossing, there are many options for going to Hanoi. You can take a shared taxi, bus or train, which can cost approximately 100,000 VND. The crossing is only open from early morning to 6 PM so you should plan your trip accordingly.

The other train crossing is located at Lao Cai, northwest Vietnam. The Chinese side of the border is the town of Hekou. Train service is only available on Vietnam's side of the border.

Organized Tours

Tourists who want to see more sights in a short time or those who are planning to visit specific places may want to consider joining organized tours. Tour packages usually include airfare, accommodation, excursions, and local travel. While tours are often more expensive than arranging your travel independently, the price difference is usually worth the convenience and the fact that you can cover more grounds. Tour duration varies and can last from several days to a few weeks.

Another option is to make arrangements with a local tour operator in major cities and tourist hubs. You can do this before your arrival or on the first few days of your stay. Locally arranged tours are generally cheaper than tour packages offered outside Vietnam but remember to transact only with reputable companies.

Chapter 6 - Getting Around

Most travels around Vietnam occur on the roads, which, on the whole, are decent enough insofar as surface is concerned. Vietnam's notoriously busy and narrow roads as well as lack of discipline among many drivers contribute on a large part to many accidents. Although things have changed much in recent years, there is still room for improvement and fine tuning.

By Plane
Getting around Vietnam by plane is a great time saver and something you should consider if you wish to cover more grounds in a shorter period.

At present, there are four airlines offering domestic flights in Vietnam: Vietnam Airlines, Jetstar, Air Mekong, and Viet Jet. Vietnam Airlines is the top player in terms of quality, routes and timeliness. Jetstar usually offers cheaper rates than Vietnam Airlines but passenger often complain of flight delays. If you're going to places like Qui Nhon, Pleiku, Phu Quoc, Dalat, or Con Dao, you may want to try Air Mekong, a new airline. VietJet only serves passengers from Hanoi to Ho Chi Minh and back.

Here is a list of Vietnam's domestic airports:

- Buon Ma Thuot Airport
- Ca Mau Airport
- Can Tho Airport
- Chu Lai Airport
- Con Dao Airport
- Da Lat Airport
- Dien Bien Phu Airport

- Dong Hoi Airport
- Hai Phong Airport
- Hue Airport
- Phu Quoc Airport
- Plieku Airport
- Qui Nhon Airport
- Rach Gia Airport
- Vinh Airport
- Tuy Hoa Airport

By Bus

Open-tour Buses
Most tourist journeys on buses are facilitated by privately operated companies specializing on tours. Popularly known as open-tour buses, these vehicles do not start out from bus stations but on the offices of the operators. They travel from Hanoi to Ho Chi Minh, but passengers are free to stop at other destinations along the way such as Nha Trang, Hoi An, Da Lat, Mui Ne, Hué, Ninh Binh, and Da Nang . This practice makes sightseeing more economical and time-efficient for tourists. Although buses are fine, these can get too crowded. The more expensive open-tour buses have on-board toilet but most don't and have to pull in every several hours at restaurants along the road. It's best to bring your own snack as many of these restaurants have mediocre food.

Private buses usually have fixed timetables, limited seats and air-conditioning. Some open-tour journeys take place overnight. Travellers who are on budget prefer to take the overnight trip to cut their hotel expenses. Most overnight buses provide sleeper berths but sleep is often a precious commodity when travelling in Vietnamese roads and with Vietnamese drivers on the wheel. Mai Linh and Hoang Long are two of the most reputable bus operators.

Bus rates vary widely depending on the operator and on the stops you want to make along the way. You will have the option to make a firm booking at the start or buy an open-dated ticket, which will require you to book your onward travel one or two-days in advance to secure your seat. An alternative is to buy separate tickets from each stop as you go along the trip.

State buses
The government is gradually upgrading state buses by replacing old models with air-conditioned buses. If you're on a hurry, you'll get frustrated with the frequent bus stops to pick up passengers along the way or allow passengers to take their meals or snacks. If you happen to ride on old models, you will most likely suffer breakdowns on the road that can delay your trip considerably.

It's best to buy your tickets at the bus station where the rates are indicated. The fare is supposed to be indicated on the ticket but if you're going to catch the bus in some other places particularly in the more remote areas, you may be charged a different amount just because you happen to be a tourist.

By Rail
As more travellers now prefer the services of open-tour buses, train patrons have declined considerably. Train travel, however, has its own advantages. You may want to consider taking a ride to have a good feel of the countryside and Vietnamese culture. In addition, since it is running on its own track, you are less likely to be involved in collision with

speeding vehicles, trucks or motorbikes that are actual risks particularly if you're travelling in Highway 1.

The single-track 2,500-kilometer rail network is run by the Vietnam Railways. The rail network starts at the Ho-Chi Minh City and ends at the Chinese border. Although they are being gradually improved, most trains are dated and run painfully slow.

Local transport

Getting around in major cities is much easier with plenty of good options such as taxis and bus services. When travelling to other places, however, two or three-wheeled vehicles are the norm for moving around.

Xe om

The most common mode of transportation is the motorbike taxi called xe om. If you don't mind riding at the back of the motorbike driver, xe oms are cheap and ubiquitous. Rates are never fixed but on the average, the shortest trip will cost around 5,000VND and you can still bargain. When negotiating, make sure that you're talking about the same currency. Write down what was agreed upon and give exact fare. Expect the rate to go up after dark.

Motorbikes may be rented on a daily basis at an average rate of $7 per day but you can haggle and ask for a discount specially if you're renting the machine for several days. It can be a time-saving and cost-efficient option for sightseeing. Riders are required to wear helmets.

Cyclo

The cyclo is a three-wheeled rickshaw that has been replaced in many places by the xe om. They are now more commonly found in tourist areas.

Taxis

Taxis are now very common in all major cities and larger towns and a cheap way to get to your destination. Taxis charge 12,000-15,000VND per kilometer and are mostly metered. Some drivers, however, need persuasion to use the meter while some will take their passengers to longer routes to charge more. Opt for the more reputable and reliable taxi companies to avoid unsavory situations. Mai Linh Taxi, Vinasun Taxi, and Hanoi taxi are the three most popular taxi companies in Vietnam.

Mai Linh Taxi: Tel: 38.23.23.23
Vinasun Taxi: Tel: 38.27.27.27
Hanoi Taxi: Tel: 38.53.53.53

Chapter 7 - Accommodation

The advent of the internet and online booking has made a traveller's search for hotels and accommodations easier than ever but the deluge of information and diverse reviews from fellow travellers and biased sites can make the task pretty challenging. With a good dose of good old common sense and focused research, however, it is possible to find and book a hotel/hostel in Vietnam which meets all expectations.

In general, the quality of accommodation in Vietnam is more or less exceptional. The industry is rising and new buildings are being constructed to meet the needs of the steadily growing number of international visitors. The fierce competition among hotels is keeping rates down and the service standards up. Whether you're on the lookout for luxury hotels or low cost accommodations, there is a wide array of options to suit your budget. Most hotels run promotions where great discounts can be enjoyed by travellers who book their stay directly with the hotel.

Booking your stay in advance is necessary especially during major holidays like the Tet Festival. You can ask assistance from a tourist booth staff in the international airports in Hanoi and Ho Chi Minch city who will gladly call a hotel to reserve a room. It's not advisable to ask for advice from taxi or cyclo drivers when choosing a hotel as they may just refer you to a hotel with which they have a prior arrangement for referral fees. Some go to the extent of telling their passenger that the hotel of their choice is either closed or full. Be aware that there are many hotels with identical names and it's important to write down the full and exact address and present it to the driver.

Before booking a hotel room, ask to be allowed to see a range of rooms as each establishment may have varying standards or room types. If you want a room with a view, make sure you're getting one by asking and checking. If you're particular about bed arrangement, check if the room has the type of bed you need as the hotel, specially the budget ones, may have a different standard for what is a single bed, twin bed, double bed, queen-sized or king-sized bed.

Hotels usually ask for the passport upon check-in for identification and reporting with local authorities. Some hotels return the passport on the same night while some hotels will keep the passport for security purposes during your stay. If you're anxious about leaving your passport with them, just tell the staff that you will need the passport for banking or visa transactions. Many hotels now accept photocopies of visa pages and a picture in lieu of the original passport.

All hotels charge 10% VAT and most high class establishments add an average of $5 service charge. It's important to ask if the quoted rate includes both charges. Nearly all hotels include breakfast in the room rate which can be as simple as a cup of coffee or tea and bread with jam. The more opulent hotels offer buffet breakfast for those who are willing to splurge more. Room rates are usually dependent on demand and it is always a good idea to bargain.
When negotiating with the front desk staff, make sure that you're talking about the same thing. Ask whether the rate is per room or per person. You're more likely to drive a good bargain when booking a stay for several nights.

Hotel security is a typical concern among guests. Your documents, wallet, traveller's checks and other valuables should be with you at all times. Many mid-range to high-range hotels provide a safety deposit box in every room which you can use while in the hotel. Other hotels allow their guests to leave their things in a locked cabinet or drawer or in some cases, in a common safe at the reception. It's a good idea to bring extra padlocks to secure your room or a cabinet inside the room. If you must leave your belongings or documents at the front desk, make sure to put them in a sealed envelope. Don't forget to ask for a receipt or its equivalent.

Hygiene can be a serious concern if you're staying in a super budget hotel where rooms are not maintained and cleaned regularly and where cockroaches, ants and rats are scavenging freely. You can minimize health risk by disposing your trash elsewhere or not bringing in sugary drinks and food. When travelling with children, you have to be really careful about choosing the type of accommodations. Newer hotels are usually much cleaner than older ones and the price difference is often worth the peace of mind.

Hotels in Ho Chi Minh City, Hanoi and other big cities usually offer laundry and dry cleaning services. Some hotels provide ironing facilities in each room. Avoid giving sensitive garments as clothes are usually scrubbed vigorously by hand.

Prostitution is alive and well in Vietnam. In some places, it's not uncommon for Western men to receive phone calls or visitors during the night.

Chapter 8 - Festivals and Cultural Events

Nearly all festivals and cultural events in Vietnam are based on the lunar calendar but in recent years, they have joined the world in celebrating holidays based on the Gregorian or Christian calendar.

The Tet Festival (1st, 2nd, and 3rd day of the Lunar Year)

The Lunar New Year Festival or the Tet Festival is one of the most important holidays in Vietnam. It is a three-day celebration of the Vietnamese and Chinese New Year and a time for Vietnamese to honor their ancestors, visit their relatives and wish for good fortune. Officially, the festival is held on the first, second and third day of the Lunar Calendar, which usually fall between January and February. Traditionally, however, the Vietnamese people spend one week to about a month to celebrate the annual event.

Tet Trung Thu or the Mid-Autumn Moon Festival (15th day of 8th lunar month)

The Mid-Autumn Moon Festival is one of the two most important festivals in Vietnam. This ancient festival dates back to 15,000-20,000 years ago and revolves around children and families. Moon cake is often served as part of the celebration.

Hue Festival

This is a biennial festival held in the month of April every even year. It celebrates the cultural heritage of Hue City and Vietnam with traditional games, art performances and depiction of historical events.

New Years Day (Worldwide celebration)
1 January

Anniversary - founding of the Communist Party of Vietnam
3 February - public holiday

Liberation Day (South Vietnam and Saigon)
30 April

Labor Day (Worldwide holiday)
1 May

Ho Chi Minh's birthday
19 May

Hung King Temple Festival
10th day of the 3rd Lunar month

Buddha's Birthday
8th day of the 4th lunar month
This is a public holiday to commemorate Buddha's birth, enlightenment, and death.

Wandering Souls Day
15th day of the 7th lunar month

Vietnamese celebrate the day by burning fake money to honor their deceased relatives and by offering food in their house altars for the souls of the dead who are believed to wander in the homes of their offspring on this special day.

National Day
2 September

Anniversary of the death of Ho Chi Minh
3 September

Birthday of Confucius
28th day of 9th lunar month

The day is celebrated in Confucian temples in Vietnam.

Christmas Day (worldwide holiday)
25th December

Chapter 9 - Survival Guide and Safety Tips

Vietnam is a country on the rise and while it is a relatively safe country, it's important to take precautions to avoid health hazards, petty crimes and accidents.

A discreet money belt will be useful in carrying your passport, travellers' checks and cash. A padlock will be handy for securing your luggage on buses and trains and for locking windows and door. Keep a photocopy of your important documents like passport and insurance policy details.

Keep an eye on your valuables and secure them with a cable lock while on a train or a bus.

Avoid ostentatious display of wealth and forego flashy jewelry and watches. Don't wear cameras hanging around your neck to avoid being targeted for snatching.

Refuse to accept food and drinks from strangers as there have been stories of tourists being drugged and robbed.

When walking on the streets, be aware that motorcycle drivers often use the pavements to beat traffic jams, putting the lives of pedestrians in danger.

Since the pavements are widely used as parking areas for motorbikes and as a place to eat and sit on, be ready to walk alongside traffic in the streets.

To minimize health and stomach problems, avoid milk drinks, smoothies and spicy street food.

Ask permission before taking pictures. Some museums require visitors to leave their cameras and bags at the reception.

Ho Chi Minh is rather notorious for pickpockets, bag-snatchers and con artists. Thieves sometimes use kids and old women as decoy. Avoid taking cyclos after dark and walking alone outside District 1 and District 3.

Petty crimes involving drugs and prostitution are likewise rampant in Nha Trang.

Dress modestly when visiting shrines and religious sites.

Public display of affection is frowned upon.

Chapter 10 - Travel Essentials

Money
The unit of currency is the Vietnamese Dong, which is variably abbreviated as "VND", "d", or "đ" after the amount. The exchange rate as of the day of writing is 22,487.50 for each US Dollar and 34,060.13 for each British Pound. While Vietnamese laws require the use of Dong for local sales and purchase transactions, almost all shops accept dollars. However, if you want to make the most out of your money, it's better to have it changed to the local currency and use the dong for paying your purchases.

When changing currencies, request for a good mix of denominations as you may find it difficult to change larger bills in remote areas. Hotels, travel agents and jewelry shops usually offer better exchange rates than banks but you must exercise caution when using alternative places for changing your currency.

Bill denominations are 500d, 1000d, 2000d, 5000d, 10,000d, 20,000d, 100,000d, and 200,000d. Vietnamese coins, though rarely seen, come in denominations of 200d, 500d, 1000d, 2000d, and 5000d.

There are many ATMs providing 24-hour service in Hanoi, Ho Chi Minh City and other tourist centers but bringing US dollars in hard cash as backup is advised. ATMs can dispense up to two million dong per withdrawal with a corresponding local service charge of 20,000-30,000 dong for every transaction. This is on top of whatever fees your bank may charge. Major banks will change other currencies, including

UK pound, Euros, Canadian dollars, Australian dollars, Swiss franc, Singapore dollar, Hong Kong dollars, and Thai baht.

Credit cards are increasing acceptance in major tourist areas and the main cities. The bigger hotels, fine dining restaurants and hospitals invariably take major credit cards for payments but travelers are advised to inquire of any surcharge, which can range from 2.5% to 5% of your bill. Traveler's checks denominated in US dollars may be changed to cash in some of the banks in the country's major cities or towns. Banks usually don't charge commissions if the check is converted directly to dong but may charge from 2-4% commission if the check is cashed into US dollars.

Language
You can find English speakers in places where there are tourist services but communication can be a problem in other areas. The Vietnamese language is basically tonal and it is not an easy language to learn. Thankfully, it uses the Roman alphabet, which makes it a lot easier to read directions and remember captions, street names and other signs. French is still spoken by a dwindling number of elderly and educated citizens.

Time
Vietnam's time is 7 hours ahead of the GMT.

Electricity
Vietnam's electricity supply is 220 volts and sockets used are mostly round 2-pin. Many large hotels use 3 -square pin sockets. Power supply is occasionally erratic.

Postal services

Postal services in the major towns are efficient and reliable and mail delivery in and out of Vietnam typically takes only about eight to ten days. Post offices are open daily from 6:30am to 9pm. Most small post offices are closed during noon break and on weekends. Depending on your location, regular postal services in other parts of the country can take about four days to a month. The Express Mail Service expedites mail delivery time significantly and is available for many overseas destinations as well as to specific local destinations. Overseas rates are also reasonable. Postal offices charge around US$32 for mails weighing 250 grams or less.

If you're planning to send parcels from Vietnam, don't bother wrapping since it will be inspected and evaluated for customs liability. Customs employees themselves will do the wrapping after the inspection and you will be charged at least 30,000 dong for the entire process. Illegal items will be seized at the customs. The cheapest option for sending your parcel is surface mail, which usually takes between one to four months delivery.

Major post offices offer poste restante services for tourists who do not want to have their mail delivered to their address in Vietnam. To collect poste restante or general mails, a passport is usually required for identification. The post office charges a minimal fee per mail item. The recipient has two months to collect the mail before returning it to the sender.

Operating hours

Basic business hours are from 7:30 to 11:30 am and 1:30 to 4:30 pm with 2 hours lunch break. Offices are generally close on Sundays. State-owned banks, private banks and government offices operate from Monday to Friday. Most banks are open from 8 to 11:30 in the morning and 1:00 to 4:00 in the afternoon but there are banks with longer operating hours and city branches that are open at noon. Some banks operating in tourist centers are open during weekends and operate on extended office hours during weekdays.

Market stalls and shopping centers are open daily and operate until 8pm or longer in the big cities. Most stalls and private shops are closed during noon for lunch breaks and siesta. Most museums are closed at least once a week on Mondays and operating hours are commonly from 8 to 11:00 in the morning and 2 to 4:00 in the afternoon.

Pagodas and temples are open seven days a week with noon breaks and accepts visitors until the late evening.

Maps
If you're planning to do some motorbike touring, you can find more detailed maps in bigger bookstores in Ho Chi Minh City and Hanoi. The Vietnam Ecotourism Map published by the Fauna and Flora International provides important information on national parks and other interesting places with environmental significance.

Internet
Although it is still under monitoring and control by the government, internet access has vastly improved in recent years and broadband services are now available in Ho Chi Minh and Hanoi. You can also find internet cafés in almost every town.

Many hotels now offer WIFI access for free. Internet service in remote places tends to be more expensive and much slower.

Internet rates in major cities average about 100 dong per minute.

Mobile Phones
Mobile internet and mobile phone charges in Vietnam are among the lowest in the world. The cheapest and simplest way to connect using your mobile phone is to buy a prepaid sim card, which often carries call credits equivalent to about 2 to 3 times the purchase price of prepaid sim cards. You can top your load using prepaid cards and call your home country for as low as 4,000d per minute. Domestic calls cost about 1,300d per minute. The three major mobile service providers are Vinaphone, Mobilefone, and Viettel. Mobile operators offer 3G/HSDPA service all over the country for as low as 50,000d for 1 G data as a special package rate that requires registration prior to usage.

While current regulations require prepaid mobile phone users to register before activation of phone service, you need not fret too much about this regulation as most shops sell pre-activated sim cards to save themselves and their customers the trouble at the time of purchase. The sim cards are usually registered using fictitious names.

Using your home country's mobile provider is usually far more expensive than using local mobile phone services.

Traveling with children
Touring Vietnam with children can be a fun and enjoyable experience but it can also be challenging. Children are more sensitive to unsanitary conditions and unfamiliar foods and their stomach may take longer to adjust. If they do get sick, keep their fluid intake up to avoid dehydration. Health care facilities outside the main cities of Ho Chi Minh and Hanoi

offer basic services and you should be prepared to spend on possible medical evacuation should the need arise.

You can find low cost hotels with rooms that have three or four single beds. Many mid-range to high-range hotels allow children below twelve years of age to stay at their parents' room free of charge.

When moving around the country, the trains offer the most comfortable and safer travel options as long and crowded bus journeys are usually difficult for young children. Children can enjoy reduced fares on planes, tour buses and trains.

Travelers with special requirements

There are few provisions for travelers with disabilities and if you happen to be one, you will have to rely mostly on your own devices. You will need to inform the hotel, tour agency and the airline well ahead of time to make sure that your request will be accommodated.

Hiring a private car or taxis can make traveling more convenient for you but the uneven pavements and rough roads may pose real difficulties.

Newly-built opulent hotels offer specially adapted rooms but you will have to reserve in advance as these rooms are few. When booking accommodations in other hotels, your best option is to find a room in the ground floor or a hotel with an elevator.

There are few buildings in Vietnam with ramps and lifts and people with disabilities may find it really challenging to move around.

There are tour agents that offer customized tours for people with special needs and you may find it more convenient to book a tour with them. This is, of course, a more expensive option.

Section 2
Travel Guide to Major Destinations

Chapter 11 - Ho Chi Minh City

Ho Chi Minh City is Vietnam's largest and most energetic city. A lively and oftentimes frenetic hub of culture and commerce, visitors are often carried by the vitality it breathes into its residents. During the day, it is a vibrant city of wonderful discoveries. At night, it is wide awake with a slew of restaurants offering great food and bars to entertain visitors who are looking for fun and exciting adventures.

More than three million motorbikes pass by the lively and busy streets of the city. It is one of the most-populated metropolitan centers in the world, with nearly eight million people.

Most locals still fondly call Ho Chi Minh City by its old name, Saigon. Saigon was the capital of the former French colony while Ho Chi Minh City was the capital of South Vietnam until the reunification in 1975.

Ho Chi Minh has risen from the ravages of war to become a fast growing city and a major tourist attraction in Vietnam. Its universities and colleges attract foreign enrollees who are impressed by the quality of education in many learning institutions.

Modern luxury shopping malls and supermarket chains have sprung up in the city in the last decades making Ho Chi Minh the commercial hub of Vietnam.

Like Hanoi, Ho Chi Minh is a city with a glorious past. As a former French capital, it is heavily influenced by the style and culture of its past colonizer. Visitors are often fascinated by the elegant and impressive colonial buildings and tree-lined boulevards.

Shopping

Shopping is one of the highlights of a visit to this burgeoning city. The variety of shopping experience makes a visit to the commercial areas of Ho Chi Minh a truly unforgettable experience. From large shopping malls to street shops, you're bound to find items at a fraction of their price elsewhere.

Ben Thanh Market

Ben Thanh, one of the oldest and busiest landmarks in the city, offers authentic Vietnamese shopping experience with the great selection of interesting items. It's a great place to buy souvenirs, handicrafts, Vietnamese arts, bamboo arts, luggage, clothes, watches, textile, fruits and spices. The market is big and is usually crowded with shoppers out to score a big bargain. There are more than 20 eating stalls in the area that give visitors a chance to have a taste of Vietnamese cuisine. The best time to go is in the early morning when it's cooler and there are plenty of fresh produce. The market is open until 11 in the evening.

Vincom Center

Vincom Center is the largest shopping mall in the city. The 5-storey mall boasts of more than 250 shops in its two buildings. If you're looking for the latest trends, you'll find international brand names for fashion, jewelry, shoes, toys and make-up products. A dining area offers a wide selection of food including local delicacies, Chinese food, and Western fare. The Game Center is the biggest in the city. Young children will be entertained at "The Fairy Garden".

Opening Hours :   09:00 AM – 10:00 PM
Phone: (+84 8) 3936 9999

Binh Tay Market

The Binh Tay Market is a major attraction in Cholon, Chinatown. The usually crowded market offers a great assortment of textiles, handicrafts, fresh produce, lacquer ware, and other Vietnamese and Chinese goods.

Saigon Square

Saigon square is the place to go for shoppers who are looking for great bargains in shoes, clothes, swimwear, luggage, accessories, textiles and jewelry. A great variety of items are sold at wholesale prices in this two-storey arcade.

Location: District 1, corner of Le Loi and Nam Kỳ Khởi
Opening Hours: 08:00 AM to 10:00 PM

Diamond Plaza

Diamond Plaza is surrounded by famous tourist attractions like the April 30th Park and the Notre Dame Cathedral. It is a big mall that remained popular among shoppers despite the emergence of new shopping malls like Vincom. Its food court offers multiple dining experience including fast food choices like Pizza Hut or KFC. The gaming center and entertainment areas offer a lot of fun and family-friendly activities. There's a cinema showing Western movies with Vietnamese subtitles and a modern bowling center.

Operating hours: 09:30 AM – 10:30 PM (shopping center)
                    09:30 AM -1:00 AM (Cinema and Superbowl)
Location: 34 Le Duan Street, District 1
Phone: (+84 8) 3825 7750

Parkson Plaza

Parkson Plaza offers a compact shopping experience in its four-storey building in District 1. Products are in the mid-range to high-range. It has other branches in the city, including one at District 5 which boasts of a modern cinema.

Operating hours:	9:30AM to 10:00 PM
Address:	45 Le Thanh Ton Street, District 1
Phone:	+84 (0) 8 3827 763

Boutique Stores

Khaisilk
Address:	107 Dong Khoi Street, District 1
Phone :	(+84 8) 38291146

Nguyen Cong Tri
Address:	194 Nguyen Dinh Chieu Street, District 3
Phone:	(+84 8) 39306757

Magonn
Address:	41 Hai Bà Trưng, District 1
Phone:	(+84 8) 38 220649

Massimo Ferrari
Address:	42A1 Tran Quoc Thao, District 3
Phone:	(+84 8) 3930 6212

My Way Deco
Address:	13 Nguyen Thiep Street, District 1
Phone:	(+84 8) 3823 8532

Dogma
Address: 1st Floor, 43 Ton That Thiep, District 1
Phone: (+84 8) 3821 8272

DMC by Do Manh Cuong
Address: 213 Lý Tự Trọng, District 1

Minh Hanh
Address: Vietnam Designers House - 161A Hai Ba Trung, District 3
Phone: (+84 8) 3521 0641

Where to Stay

Ho Chi Minh City is the most-visited place in Vietnam. Tourists looking or accommodation need not look farther as there are many hotels near the Tan Son Nhat airport. The airport is about 7 kilometers away from the city center. Visitors are most likely to find a hotel that suits their budget, needs and preferences as there is a great diversity in prices, quality and service offerings. Hotels in District 1, the location of several landmarks and tourist attractions, receive the most bookings. Hotels in other crowded areas like the China Town or Cho Lon and District 7 get their fair share of visitors.

Low Range to Mid-Range Accommodations

Ly Loan (Low range)

Address: 241/11/2 Pham Ngu Lao, District 1.
Phone: (08) 3837 0067
Email: phphuong90@yahoo.com

Ly Loan is a guest house offering large, clean, and air-conditioned rooms equipped with free Wi-Fi, refrigerator, furniture and bathtubs. Guests can use the computer in the common hall for free. Advanced booking is recommended especially during peak season.

Rates:
Standard (Single)   13 USD
Standard (Double)   16 USD
Additional $2 for front rooms with balcony

Ngoc Thao Guesthouse (low range)

Address: 241/4 Pham Ngu Lao, District 1
Phone: (08) 8337 0273;

The Ngoc Thao Guesthouse offers 12 rooms at varying prices only one of which is an air-conditioned mixed dorm with balcony which is good for 8 persons. Each room has air-conditioning, and comes equipped with a cable TV and a ceiling fan.

Rates:
Dorm (air-con)   8 USD
Standard - Single   17 USD
Standard - Double   18 USD

The Long Hostel (Low Range)
Address: 373/10 Pham Ngu Lao, District 1
Phone: (08) 3836 0184;

There's only one dorm room in this hostel and it's good for five people. There are, however, air-conditioned private rooms with a private bath and television and these are clean and well-maintained. Fee includes breakfast.

Rates:
Dorm air-conditioned   7US$
Standard-double   18US$

Saigon Backpackers' Hostel
Address: 373/20 Pham Ngu Lao, District 1. T: (08) 3837 0230
Website: http://saigonbackpackershostels.com
Email: sgbackpackershostel@gmail.com

Saigon Backpackers' Hostel offer air-conditioned rooms with free Wi-Fi, tea or coffee, breakfast, and a 24-hour desk. The entertainment area has a large flat screen TV and guests can use the PS3 for free. You can also use the kitchen and the kitchen equipment.

Rates
Dorm Room	8 USD
Superior double room	25 USD
Superior twin room	28 USD
Superior triple room	35 USD
Superior family room	35 USD
Connecting room	40 USD

The Spring Hotel – Saigon   (3-Star)
Address: 44 Lê Thánh Tôn, District 1, Hồ Chí Minh, Vietnam
Phone: +84 8 3829 7362

The Spring Hotel Saigon is a sparkling boutique hotel designed to meet the standards of foreign visitors at incredibly modest rates. It is a 45-room hotel, which offers great location, fine services, English-speaking staff and amenities including free private parking, free WIFI, free air-conditioning, free fax, photocopying and newspaper. Rooms are equipped with cable television, a safe and a minibar. Ironing facilities and a hairdryer are provided. The hotel offers currency exchange and baggage storage services. The Spring Hotel is very near the Opera House, Saigon River, Vincom Shopping Center, Parkson, shops, and popular restaurants and only about 6.4 kilometers from the Tan Son Nhat Airport. For an additional fee, the hotel can provide an airport shuttle service. Pets are not allowed.

Rate: 39-49

A& Em 5 Hotel (3-Star)

Address: 150 Le Thanh Ton Str, Dist 1, Ho Chi Minh City, Vietnam
Distance: 0.45km to city center

Though its facilities are not that modern, the hotel is suitable for an average traveler's needs. Hotel guests can enjoy free WIFI, free buffet breakfast, air-conditioned rooms with twin bed, bath tub, TV with cable channels, and other essentials at a very affordable rate. If traveling with children, one child not older than seven can get a free pass if he/she stays in the parents' room. However, he will not be entitled to free breakfast. Airport shuttle service is available. Pets are not allowed.

Check In: 2:00PM, Check Out: 12:00PM

Rate   Average of 38$

A& Em 1 Le Prince Hotel (3-star)

Rate: 38$ Average
Address: 132 Ly Tu Trong Street, District 1, Ho Chi Minh City, Vietnam
Distance: 0.55km to city center

The hotel offers clean and well-maintained rooms with free air-conditioning, Wi-Fi, private parking, baggage storage, business center, elevator, 24-hour front desk, English-speaking staff, and other essential amenities. The hotel offers free stay for all children under 6 years old provided they will be using existing beds on their parents' room. Pets are allowed with no additional charges.

Check In: 2:00PM, Check Out: 12:00PM

Saigon Star Hotel (3-star)

Address: 204 Nguyen Thi Minh Khai Street, District 3 Ho Chi Minh City
Tel: (84.8) 39306290/39306296 (hotline: 39306291)
Fax: (84.8) 39306300

Saigon Star Hotel is located across the City Cultural Park, near the Reunification Palace and the Notre Dame Church. The spacious rooms are tastefully furnished with complete facilities. The hotel offers competitive rates for three types of accommodations: superior, deluxe, and suite. Hotel fees cover free daily breakfast buffet, purified water, coffee, tea, welcome drink, free Wi-Fi in rooms and in common areas, and free use of PC at the Lobby. Hotel guests may avail of city tour, tour of the Cu Chi Tunnel, and airport drop off. Interested travelers are advised to inquire about seasonal promotions and great discounts.

Regular Hotel Rates:

Superior   Twin/Double, 1,575 VND   Single 1,365 VND
Deluxe   Twin/Double, 1,695 VND   Family, 2,050 VND, Single, 1500 VND
Suite   Twin/Double, 2,415 VND   Single, 1,720 VND

Website: www.saigonstarhotel.com.vn
E-mail: saigonstarhotel@hcm.vnn.vn

Ha Hien Hotel (3-star)

Address: 145-147 Ly Tu Trong Street, District 1, Ho Chi Minh City
Website: http://hahienhotel.com.vn
Phone: 848.3823.4363
Fax: 848.3823.4359

Ha Hien Hotel offers a comfortable and pleasant stay at its hotel rooms at a rate that is very light on the pocket. It is located near major attractions such as the Fine Art Museum, Ben Thanh Market, Reunification Palace and The Opera House. Each room is provided with mineral water, coffee and tea. Amenities include air conditioning and satellite/cable TV.

You may book directly with the hotel if you want to get the best rates. Here are the average rates quoted by travel agencies (inclusive of booking fees):

Standard	$30/night
Deluxe	$39/night
Triple Deluxe	$52/night
Suite Double	$63/night
Suite Quad	$75-$82/night

Check In: 2:00PM / Check Out: 12:00PM

Mid-Range to High Range Accommodations:

Hotel Sofitel Saigon Plaza Ho Chi Minh City (5-star)

Address: Central Plaza Building, 17 Lê Duẩn, Ho Chi Minh City, Vietnam
Phone: +84 8 3824 1555

Sofitel Saigon Plaza offers luxurious accommodations to discriminating travelers who won't settle for anything less. The hotel is located near major tourist attractions, shops, business areas and entertainment centers. Amenities include a swimming pool, fitness center, bars and high-speed Wi-Fi access. On-site dining is available.

Rate: 130$ up (inclusive of booking fee)

Rex Hotel Saigon

Address: 141 Nguyen Hue Blvd, Ho Chi Minh City, Vietnam
E-mail: rexhotel@rex.com.vn
Website: http://www.rexhotelvietnam.com
Phone: (8 48) 38292185
Fax: (8 48) 38296536

Rex Hotel Saigon is a heritage hotel that has seen many historical events in the city in over eighty years of operations. One of the main landmarks of Ho Chi Minh City, Rex Hotel combines luxurious modern facilities with traditional Vietnamese hospitality to provide its guests a memorable stay. The hotel offers 286 rooms equipped with modern facilities and equipment including satellite/cable TV, Wi-Fi access, refrigerator, air-conditioning, separate bathroom with shower and bathtub, microwave oven, mini kitchen, ironing board, and a mini bar. Other amenities include two outdoor swimming pool, tennis court, parking, luxury spa and fitness center, currency exchange, safety deposit box, 24-hour front desk with English-speaking staff and a business center equipped with the latest communications equipment and internet access.

Travelers may book directly with the hotel to avail of discounts of up to 5%. Here are the average room rates quoted by travel companies:

Deluxe	$105
Premium	$145
Rex Suite	$147
Governor Suite	$220
Executive Suite	$370
President Suite	$900

Check In: 2:00PM / Check Out: 12:00PM

New World Hotel Saigon (5-star)

Address:	76 Le Lai Street, District 1, Ho Chi Minh City, Vietnam
Phone:	+84 8 3822 8888 Fax: +84 8 3823 0710
Distance:	0.46km to city center

The New World Hotel Saigon offers 533 luxurious rooms fully equipped with modern amenities, the largest in the city. It is a popular wedding reception venue for the upper class of Ho Chi Minh. Large windows in every room offer hotel guests a sweeping view of the city. It is conveniently located near the Notre Dame Church and the Tao Dan Park. The TSN airport is a mere 20-minute drive. Each room is equipped with a flat-screen TV, tea and coffee-maker, mini-bar, and a private bathroom with bathtub and walk-in shower. Guests can use the swimming pool, fitness center, tennis court and Wi-Fi access.

Rates with booking fees:

Superior: $135-$155/night   Deluxe: $145-$159/night

Park Hyatt Saigon

Address: 2 Lam Son Square, District 1 Ho Chi Minh City
Phone: +84 8 3824 1234

The newly-renovated hotel offers modern facilities and 245 lavish and comfortable hotel rooms and suites in a prime area in Ho Chi Minh City. It is within walking distance of the Reunification Palace, Central Post Office, and the Notre Dame Cathedral and about 2.4 kilometer from Saigon Train Station. The TSN airport is a mere 45-minute drive. Guests can use the hotel's 24-hour gym and round-the-clock room service. Amenities include free Wi-Fi, air-conditioning, parking, mini bar, and satellite/cable TV.

Check-in time: 02:00PM / Check-out time: 12:00PM

The hotel offers as much as 20% discounts for guests who book directly on Hyatt.com website. Here are the average Rates quoted by booking companies (inclusive of booking fees):

Standard Room	$335-$380/night
Deluxe King	$499-$543/night
Suite King	$690-$735/night
Executive Suite	$920-$965/nigh

Where to Eat

Ho Chi Minh City is a haven of fine restaurants offering French, Chinese and local cuisine. The street food scene, however, is undeniably an inextricable aspect of Vietnamese dining experience. Street food and snack booths permeate every alley, district and neighborhood in Saigon. Thousands of eateries serve delicious yet cheap food in an open air restaurant environment.

If you want to experience street food dining in Saigon, head out to the following streets for an unforgettable experience:

Van Kiep Street
Van Kiep Street is at the border of Phu Nuan and Binh Thanh districts. Here you can find over a hundred eateries offering dozens of Vietnamese local dishes including phở, chè, bánh mì, bánh canh cua, bún mắm, bánh xèo, bún bò Huế, nem nướng, and bún chả. Majority of diners in this area are young Vietnamese.

Su Van Hanh Street
You can find delicious street foods in the area between Nguyễn Chí Thanh and Ngô Gia Tự streets in the long street of Su Van Hanhi in District 10. Houses in this area are small and cramped and people would rather be out on the streets than inside their abode. The street specializes in savory crepes stuffed with bean sprouts and pork called bánh xèo. One of the popular stall in this street is 004 Lô H, which has been serving the delicacy for over fourteen year. You can also find stalls offering Chinese-style noodles.

Co Giang Street

Co Giang Street offers Ho Chi Minh's backpackers and curious tourists a more authentic Vietnamese dining experience than they would get in many formal restaurants in District 1. Although it is not as crowded as the other streets, Co Giang Street never fails to attract customers because of the tempting cooking smoke of street barbeques, bubbling cauldrons and woks. A serving of bò lá lốt or grilled beef costs around 20,000 VND.

Tran Khac Chan Street

The busy Tran Khac Chan Street in District 1 is a paradise for foodies as it features about 50 food stalls and trolleys. Here you can have a taste of bánh canh cua, a slippery noodle cooked on a crab-based concoction. You probably won't be able to resist barbecued chicken with its overwhelming smoky smell.

Nguyen Thuong Hien Street

This narrow street in District 3 is well-known for seafood cooked to order. Crabs, crab claws, mussels, sea snails, scallops, clams and oysters are on the menu. This isn't just a seafood strip though as there are exotic treats that you can enjoy like duck tongue and the hủ tiếu Nam Vang noodles. Freshly-squeezed tropical fruits are also available in several stalls.

Vĩnh Khánh Street

This strip is popular for seafood among other street food delicacies. The most famous joint is Ốc Oanh, which is known for fresh seafood served in big portions and for their efficient service. What to try: spicy fried sea snails and grilled scallops. Quán BBQ Lúa features a grill-it-yourself style of dining where the diner himself grills marinated pork, beef, goat, and fish.

Where to Go

Notre Dame Cathedral
The Notre Dame Cathedral was built by the French colonists between 1863 and 1880 using bricks and materials imported from France. An imposing building highlighted by two 60-meter tall bell towers, the basilica is one of Ho Chi Minh's architectural wonders. A visit to the city will not be complete without a glimpse of this popular tourist attraction.

District 1
Location   : Bến Nghé, Quận 1, Hồ Chí Minh
Tickets   : N/A

Cho Lon (Chinatown)
Cho Lon is a small area in Ho Chi Minh, which is home to ethnic Chinese people in Vietnam. The place has drawn many visitors who are fascinated by the distinctive lifestyle and highly traditional culture of Chinese immigrants who earn their living by engaging in commercial activities like operating food stalls serving traditional food and selling household items, clothing, and handicrafts at unbelievably cheap prices. The Ben Thanh Market is the busiest, most crowded and largest trading hub in Cho Lon.

The Chinese New Year celebration or the Tet Holiday is the best time to see Cho Lon as all shops and restaurants are luxuriantly decorated with colorful lanterns as the color of red dominates the streets. The Lion Dance is traditionally performed to bring good fortune for the New Year and it is one of the most anticipated events during the festival.

District 5
Location: Cho Lon, Ho Chi Minh

Reunification Palace (Dinh Doc Lap)

The Reunification Palace is a historical witness to two turbulent wars fought by the Vietnamese people against their French and American colonists. The five-storey palace came to world consciousness on April 30, 1975 as a symbol of the fall of Saigon, the end of Vietnam War and the reunification of Vietnam when a North Vietnamese Army Tank crashed into its main gates and hoisted the communist flag on its balcony. A few minutes before the siege, palace staff members were evacuated from the rooftop as part of the biggest helicopter evacuation code-named Operation Frequent Wind.

The palace served as a workplace and presidential home to the former South Vietnam government under President Nguyễn Văn Thiệu. Its basement houses a telecommunications center, a war command room and a network of tunnels. Visitors can view the telecommunications equipment and maps on the walls of the war command room and propaganda materials on the adjacent rooms. Other interesting areas of the Palace include a card playing room on the third floor, a helipad on the rooftop, and what used to be an area for a casino and for entertaining guests on the fourth floor.

You can reach the palace by motorbike, taxi, or by walking from the main city.

District 1
Address: 135 Nam Kỳ Khởi Nghĩa, Bến Thành, Quận 1, Hồ Chí Minh
Operating hours: Open daily from 7:30-11:3AM and 1:00pm-5:00PM
Ticket: 20,000 VND
Phone: +84 8 3822 3652
Internet: www.dinhdoclap.gov.vn

Giac Lam Pagoda

Giac Lam Pagoda was built in 1744 and it is one of the oldest and most visited pagodas during the Tet Holiday celebration. The Buddhist Pagoda was declared as a national cultural and historical site in 1988. Tourists passing through the main gate will find a huge statue of Bodhisattva under a big Bodhi tree in the garden. A gift from the great monk Narada of Sri Lanka, the Bodhi tree arrived with a sample of Gautama Buddha's relics. The seven-storey high stupa was built with the intention of storing these relics. The pagoda, the tallest Buddhist tower in Ho Chi Minh City, now stores many treasured relics and bronze and wood statues of Buddha and Bodhisattva.

The Gian Lam Pagoda is just a 15-minute ride from the City Center. You can reach it by motorbike, taxi or bus. If going by bus, you can go to the Ben Thanh Bus Station and catch Bus No 27 and alight at the Lac Long Quan-Au Co.

Address:	Lac Long Quan Str., Tan Binh District, Ho Chi Minh City
Entrance:	Free
Operating hours:	6am-noon & 2-8.30pm

War Remnants Museum

The War Remnants Museum is a showcase of the cruelty and devastation of the war between Vietnam and the United States that lasted from 1961 to 1975. The museum is the storage of disturbing photographs showing the atrocities of colonialism and the trauma of military operations conducted against Vietnam, haunting and interesting artifacts, war equipment, documentations, films and collections of stories about this painful phase in Vietnam's history.

You can reach the place by taxi or motorbike. Those who prefer to take a bus can go to the Ben Thanh Bus Station and catch Bus No. 28. The museum is located at the corner between Le Quy Don St. and Vo Van Tan St.

District 3
Operating hours: 8:00-11:45 AM
                   1:30-4:45PM
Address: 28 Vo Van Tan St, Ho Chi Minh City
Phone: +84 8 3930 5587
Entrance fee: 10,000VND

Cu Chi Tunnel (Ben Dinh/Ben Duoc)
The Cu Chi tunnel network allows visitors to have a feel of what life must have been like for North Vietnamese and Viet Cong troops who used the extensive underground structure to escape heavy aerial bombings by the US troops, move around undetected, and launch their attacks on urban areas. The extensive network used to stretch from the South Vietnamese government capital to Cambodia's border. It was built with bare hands and simple tools in the 1940s during the French occupation and expanded during the Vietnam War.

The underground construction included several trapdoors and provisions for command centers, shelter, recreational center, hideaway, weapon factory, storage facility, classrooms, medical facilities and kitchens. People living in heavily-bombed places built villages on the tunnels to survive the attacks.

Tourists can view the tunnels from a park or if you're up to it, you can go down and experience firsthand how it is to crawl inside these dark tunnels.

There are two tunnel sites open to the public, the Ben Duoc and the Ben Dinh tunnel sites. The Ben Duoc site is the original network of tunnels and is less frequented by tourists as most tours are directed to the tunnels at Ben Dinh. It is farther from Ho Chi Minh City but can be reached easily by taking bus 79 for 6,000 VND. If you wish to avoid bigger crowds, consider taking a tour of Ben Duoc.

Ben Dinh is the destination of most group tours and can get really crowded. Unlike the original tunnels at Ben Duoc, the tunnel networks at Ben Dinh were specially constructed and expanded to accommodate tourists. If you're travelling on your own, you can take bus 13 for a 1.5-hour ride to Cu Chi, its final stop. The bus trip costs 7,000VND. Upon arrival at the Cu Chi Bus station, you'll have to take a 20-minute motorbike ride to the tunnel site. You can haggle with a motorbike driver to bring the fare down to about 100,000 VND. Another option is to take bus 13 and alight at a T-junction with Ben Dinh on the right and Ben Duoc on the left. The 45-minute ride costs 6,000VND. From the T-junction, you'll have to walk for about twenty minutes to reach the entrance of the Ben Dinh tunnels.

You may also find it more convenient to join a guided bus tour to the Cu Chi tunnels. Most tour buses leave at 8:00 in the morning and charge $5 for the trip and about 1.5 hours tour on the tunnel. Tour buses for Ben Dinh can get crowded at times and you may consider joining tours that provide a private car for both trips. Fees for this type of tour service range from $40 to $75.

Address:	Cu Chi
Ticket:	110,000VND at Ben Dinh
	90,000VND at Ben Duoc

Central Post Office

The Central Post Office was designed by Gustave Eiffel, the same engineer who designed the Eiffel Tower. It is one of the oldest buildings in Ho Chi Minh City, a remnant of French colonial times that has been wonderfully preserved and appreciated for its beauty and elegance.

A mixture of Renaissance, Gothic, and French influences, the building's ornate interiors, luxurious furnishings, magnificent pattern-tiled floor, and tall arch-shaped ceilings take visitors back to another place in time.

While it is one of the tourist attractions in Ho Chi Minh, the Central Post Office is also a fully-functional post office offering traditional services like mailing and selling stamps or postcards.

The Central Post Office can be reached by motorbike, taxi, or on foot from other popular tourist sites like the War Remnant Museum or the Reunification Palace. It is located near Diamond Plaza and the Notre Dame Cathedral.

District 1
Address: 2 Paris Commune Street, Ho Chi Minh City
Operating hours: 6AM-10PM

Jade Emperor Pagoda (Chua Phuoc Hai)

Jade Emperor Pagoda, one of the most important and revered shrines in Ho Chi Minh, was built by Chinese immigrants from Guangzhou province in 1909. The temple is a fine depiction of Mahayanist Buddhism which is extensively practiced in the country. Locals visit the temple to offer prayers, flowers and light joss stick and candles. Incense smoke permeates the air and gives an atmospheric feel to the pagoda. Elaborate architecture, intricate carvings, fine and lavish decorations, and statues of gods and goddesses give the place an exotic and classic ambiance.

A statute of the 'God of the Heavens', Emperor Jade Chua Ngoc Hoang, can be found in the main hall. On the left is the 'Chief of Hell', Thanh Hoang, who is supposed to send sinners to hell. Purgatory life is depicted on the elaborate wall carvings showing different forms of punishment for transgressors.

In another hall, childless couples pray and ask for the intercession of the goddess of fertility, Kim Hua, to be blessed with an offspring. On the top floor, one can see the altar of Kuan Yin, the goddess of mercy, an important part of Taoist temples.

Temple-goers visit the tortoise pond and feed the animals as part of their rituals to earn merits for their soul. It is for this pond that the temple has also come to be known as the "Tortoise Pagoda".

District 3
Operating Hours: 07:00AM – 6:00PM
Location: 73 Mai Thi Luu, District 3
Remarks: There is no entrance fee but visitors can make donations

The Cao Dai Great Temple (near Ho Chi Minh)
Cao Daism is a religion that combines the world's most powerful religions such as Christianity, Islam, Buddhism, Hinduism, Taoism, and Geniism. Jesus Christ, Buddha, Muhammad, Confucius, Julius Cesar and Joan of Arc are venerated at their temples. Its leaders and believers promote

religious tolerance all over the world. Cao Dai means "the high tower". There are about 1,000 Cao Dai temples in Vietnam.

The Cao Dai Great Temple is the main cathedral of the religion and it is located in the city of Tay Ninh, Vietnam. Its magnificent construction and colorful decorations draw both local and international tourists. The ceiling is decorated with a cloud mural while the banisters are embellished with colorful dragons. The main focal point and symbol of Cao Daism is the Divine Eye with the Ying and Yang icon.

The Cao Dai Great Temple is located near the Cambodian border in the Long Than Village of Tay Nihn and is best reached by booking a tour. Worship are held every six hours starting at midnight with daily chanting at 6:00 AM and 6:00 PM.

Visitors can view the ceremonies and take photographs from the galleries but must remove their shoes and cover their knees before entering the temple. Silence is requested while inside the temple.

Address: Hoa Thanh District

Fine Arts Museum
The Fine Arts Museum features a vast collection of art works by Vietnamese and international artists that are exhibited in three floors. The first floor showcases local and international arts while the second floor stores and displays stone art works by both Vietnamese and foreign painters, potters, and sculptors. On exhibit are paintings of leading contemporary Vietnamese artists like Do Quang Em, Diep, Nguyen Gia, Diep Minh Chau, and Trinh Cung. The third floor displays historic arts from as early as the seventh century up to the early years

of the twentieth century and features art finds from Champa and the Oc Eo archaeological site. The museum also runs the Blue Space Contemporary Art Center, which you can find near the entrance of the museum.

The yellow-white mansion, which houses the museum is a typical colonial-era building which is considered a masterpiece itself. The grand house was originally owned by a wealthy Chinese, Mr. Hoa, who was also the owner of Tu Du Hospital and the Majestic Hotel in Saigon. The mansion was converted into a museum and was officially opened to the public in 1991.

District 1
Address: 97 A- Pho Duc Chinh, Ho Chi Minh City
Ticket: Adult, 10,000 VND, Child, 3,000 VND
Phone: +838-294-441
Website: www.baotangmythuattphcm.vn

Ho Chi Minh Zoo and Botanical Gardens

Founded more than a century ago, the Ho Chi Minh Zoo and Botanical Gardens are recognized as the 8th oldest zoo in the world. More than 500 animals including exotic species are presently on exhibit in the zoo. The botanical gardens feature more than 1,800 tree and 260 plus plant species.

Families with young children will enjoy exploring the different sections of the zoo and the botanical gardens including a children's amusement area, orchid garden, plant conservation center and an animal conservation section. The place also holds a monument dedicated to the memory of Vietnamese people who perished in World War I. Lakes which form part of the site serve as habitat to tropical fishes.

To make the most out of your visit, avoid going on weekends and during peak hours when the place is extremely crowded. The best time for visit is from 10:00AM to 1:00PM. Check their website for possible offers or discounts on tickets.

If you're taking a bus, the nearest stop is at 3 Nguyen Thi Minh Khai.

Address :   Nguyen Binh Khiem, Ben Nghe, Ho Chi Minh, Vietnam
Ticket Price: 20,000 VND
Parking: 2,000 VND
Operating hours: 7:00AM to 8:00PM

Ho Chi Minh City Nightlife

The nightlife in Ho Chi Minh City varies depending on which area you are in. The city has strict rules and most places which holds live music tend to finish just after midnight. If you want to stop out until late, then the rooftop bars and the nightclubs in District 1 is where you should be. After dark, it is a smooth, sophisticated and vibrant area with people who like to dress to impress. Head down to Districts 3 and 5, and you'll discover the cheaper options, with lively bars, packed clubs and a fantastically warm atmosphere with locals. Read on to discover some of the best nightlife options in Ho Chi Minh City.

Acoustic Bar

Located in District 3, the Acoustic Bar is the place to go for rock lovers. It regularly hosts live rock bands putting on performances that will stay with you for years to come. You'll also hear a variety of rock classics being blasted out – Jimi Hendrix and The Doors to name just two, but you'll hear rock music from all time periods. Acoustic Bar is a mixture of bar, pub and café, with couches for those wanting to sit down with a coffee or tea and enjoy a conversation before full dark, as well as the standing area when night descends. There's no food options here, but the bar is full of international visitors and locals to socialize with.

Address: 6E1 Đ Ngo Thoi Nhiem, District 3.

Sax n' Art Jazz Club

If you're looking for dark and atmospheric, look no further than the Sax n' Art Jazz Club. The jazz music played here has a somewhat Vietnamese influence to it due to the local owner who also plays various traditional instruments here. Sax n' Art

Jazz Club is slightly more expensive compared to other bars in Ho Chi Minh City, and there is an extra charge with the first drink as a cover fee, but the money is well worth every cent. This is the place where the best jazz bands in the country come to play. The bar is opens seven nights a week from 7pm to midnight, with live music starting at 9pm.

Address: 28 Le Loi, District 1

Chapter 12 - Hanoi

Hanoi is the administrative capital of Vietnam. Its rich history and varied heritage are evident in the odd mix of colonial influences, modern culture, and bucolic setting. Locals and tourists seem to move in a uniform sedate pace as they bask in the beauty of French colonial architecture set amidst tranquil lakes and tree-lined boulevards. It is a scene that hasn't changed much in the past centuries. Hanoi escaped the destructive bombing by the US forces and today, the colossal mansions stand tall and proud.

The best time to visit Hanoi is from October to April but you have to take note of the winter season, which lasts from December to February. Overcast weather and low visibility can easily dampen your enthusiasm for outdoor fun and nature tripping.

Shopping Areas in Hanoi

Hang Gai Street (Silk Street)
The entire street is cramped with fashion stores, boutiques, tailors, art galleries and silk vendors.

Hanoi Weekend Night Market
Hang Dao Street, Old Quarter

The night market offers souvenirs and fashion items every Friday, Saturday, and Sunday, 7PM to 11PM.

Dong Xuan Market
Address: Dong Xuan Street, Old Quarter
Opening hours: 7AM to 7PM.

The Dong Xuan Market offers a great range of products spread over its 4-storey building. The biggest market in the Hanoi, it has wet market on the ground floor and bargain stores on the higher floors selling fabric, luggage, shirts, fashion accessories, school uniforms and a lot more at wholesale prices.

Trang Tien Plaza
Address: Trang Tien Street
Opening hours: 11AM to 8PM

The five-storey Trang Tien Plaza caters to Hanoi's elite with its huge stocks of international designer brands and imported products, including electronics and furniture. At the fifth floor, you can find excellent restaurants selling international cuisine.

Nha Tho Street
Address: 59 A Ly Thai To Street

Nha Tho Street is a small shopping spot jammed with good restaurants and fashion stores all in a 100-meter space.

Hanoi Square (Hang Da Shopping Mall)
Address: Hang Ga Street
Opening hours: 10AM to 6PM

Hanoi Square is a modern mall selling inexpensive clothes, bags, shoes and accessories. If you're buying in bulk, you can still haggle and get a nice bargain.

Hang Dau Street
Address: Hoan Kiem Lake northeast corner
Opening hours: 9AM-8PM

Hang Dau Street is famous for hundreds of shops selling cheap pairs of shoes. Most shoes are Vietnamese brands with slight defects and factory rejects. You can also find fake or imitation bags.

Where to Eat

Hanoi is home to a huge number of restaurants and eateries catering to a wide range of diners. Specialty restaurants offering international and local cuisine and the atmospheric street food strips all enhance the unique dining experience in the city. The Old quarter houses many street stalls and reasonably-priced local dishes and Western fare. The West Lake caters to gourmet food lovers while the Hoan Kiem is the location of most international restaurants and Vietnamese restaurants selling budget food.

Restaurants to try:

Pho 24
-serves Pho
Address: VinCom City Towers, Hoan Kiem
Phone: +84 4 222 5203

Tamarind Café
-serves vegetarian dishes, Vietnamese and international menu
Address: Ma May 80, Old Quarter;
Phone: +84 4 926-0580

Daluva
- serves tapa, Western, and Asian cuisines
Address: 33 To Ngoc Van Street, West Lake
Phone: +84 4 3718 5831 or +84 907 144 561

Cam Chan Quan
-serves Beggar's chicken, Vietnamese pho, noodles
Address: 108 K1 Giang Vo Street, Ba Dinh
Phone: +84 4 259 7696

Buffet Viet
-offers buffet menu with over 100 Vietnamese and international dishes
Address: No.1A, Tang Bat Ho Street, Hai Ba Trung district, Hanoi
Phone: (+84-4) 3 993 1781
Website: http://www.buffetviet.net

New Day Restaurant
-offers solid Vietnamese dining experience
Address: 72 Mã Mây, Hàng Buồm, Hoàn Kiếm, Hà Nội, Vietnam
Phone: +84 4 3828 0315

Ngoc Mai Do Restaurant
-serves a buffet of international dishes
Address: L-15, Ruby Plaza, No.44 Le Ngoc Han Street, Hai Ba Trung District, Hanoi
Phone: (+84-4) 2 220 6799

Koto Restaurant
-offers delicious Vietnamese and Western food, owned by a charity project
Address: No.59, Van Mieu Street, Dong Da District, Hanoi
Phone: (+84-4) 3 747 0337

Where to Stay

Vietnam Backpackers' Hostel Hanoi – The Original (low range)

Although it's more than a decade old, this hostel remains a favorite among backpackers. There are mixed room as well as women-only rooms all air-conditioned and with 10 wide bunks each room. Each bed has good quality mattresses and beddings, reading light and a shelf. Each room has a bathroom with separate shower and toilet. Tea/coffee and Wi-Fi are free. A free walking tour of the Old Quarter and the cathedral is provided in the morning.

Private air-conditioned rooms with en-suit bathrooms are also available and are good for three people. There are only six private rooms so it's important to inquire for availability and book as early as possible.

Rates:
Dorm	$5/bed
Private room	$25
Address:	48 Ngo Huyen, Hoan Kiem District, Hanoi
Phone:	(+84-4) 3828 5372
Website:	www.vietnambackpackerhostels.com
Email:	original@vietnambackpackerhostels.com

Central Backpackers' Hostel (low-range)

This hostel offers private rooms and dorms with air-conditioning at really cheap prices. Dorm rooms accommodate eight people in four metal framed bunks. Rooms are not that cramped as you would except and are well-maintained. Each dorm room has one bathroom with a shower. The rates come with free breakfast and internet.

Dorm rates:	5$ per bed
Room rates:	$22-25
Address:	16 Ly Quoc Su, Hanoi
Phone:	(04) 3938 1849;

The Artisan Boutique Hotel 3-star (mid range)

This hotel features modern room equipped with satellite TV, air-conditioning, in-room laptop with free Wi-Fi access, and a mini bar. It also offers currency exchange, laundry services, and a 24-hour front desk.

The Artisan Boutique Hotel is conveniently located in the Old Quarter and is only a few minutes' walk to the Hoan Kiem Lake, Ho Chi Minh Mausoleum, and the Water Puppet Theater. It is 1 kilometer away from the Hanoi Train Station and a 40-minute drive to the Noi Bai International Airport.

Average rates:

Standard room	single, $30/ double, $37
Deluxe room	single, $40/double, $47
Address:	36 Hang Trong St. Hoan Kiem Distict Hanoi Vietnam
Website:	www.goldenricehotel.com
Phone:	(+84-4)3 938 2929
Fax:	(+84-4)3 824 7449
Email:	sales@goldenricehotel.com

Maison d'Orient (Mid-range)

The hotel is conveniently located in one of the busiest tourist spots in Hanoi but it is a surprisingly peaceful and relaxing place. The lobby and rooms are understated but all rooms are equipped with flat screen TVs, bathroom, mini bar, and good quality beddings. Ginger rooms are spacious and come with a fridge, microwave, halogen stove, cooker and sink.

Average rate:	20-50
Address:	26 Ngo Huyen, Hang Trong, Hoan Kiem, Hanoi
Phone:	(04) 3938 2539
Fax:	(04) 3976 6247

Hanoi Pearl Hotel 4-star (High range)

The hotel opened for business in the middle of 2013 and is a popular choice for large tours. Its features include a fitness center, 24-hour desk, free Wi-Fi access, air-conditioning, cable TV, mini bar, coffee/tea maker, hairdryer, and a bathroom in every room. On site dining is available at Hanoi Pearl Restaurant.

On top of the excellent amenities, the hotel is conveniently located near major tourist attractions in Hanoi including the Hoan Kiem Lak, which is just a minute's walk. The hotel is about 3 minutes away from St. Joseph's Cathedral, Thang Long Water Puppet Theater, and the Ngoc Son Temple. You can also stroll and reach the Dong Xuan Market in 10 minutes. It is near restaurants and street food joints. The hotel is 30 kilometers away from the Noi Bai International Airport and airport service can be arranged.

Guests can enjoy a tasty selection of international cuisines served at Hanoi Pearl Restaurant. The Lounge & Café Terrace offers a variety of snacks and beverages. Room service option is available.

Average rates:

Superior - Single	60 USD
Superior - Double	70 USD
Deluxe- Single	70 USD
Deluxe- Double	80 USD

Address:	6 Ngo Bao Khanh, Hoan Kiem, Hanoi
Website:	www.hanoipearlhotel.com
Email:	sales@hanoipearlhotel.com
Phone:	+84 4 3938 0666 -
Fax:	+84 4 3938 0777

Golden Rice Hotel   3-star   High range

Golden Rice Hotel is a conveniently located boutique hotel in the Old Quarter where the majority of tourist sites can be found. It features free Wi-Fi, 24-hour desk, air-conditioned rooms equipped with a mini bar and 40-inch flat television. On-site dining is also provided at the Golden Rice Restaurant.

The hotel is about 5 to 10 minutes walk to the Water Puppet Theater, Temple of Literature, Vietnamese Fine Art Museum, and the Dong Xuan Market.

Average rates:

Deluxe Suite	120 USD
Superior Double	60 USD
Standard Double	50 USD

Address:	36 Hang Trong St. Hoan Kiem Dist. Hanoi Vietnam
Website:	www.goldenricehotel.com
Email:	sales@goldenricehotel.com Website:
Phone:	(+84-4)3 938 2929
Fax:	(+84-4)3 824 7449

Where to Go

Ho Chi Minh's Mausoleum

Ho Chi Minh Mausoleum houses the glass-encased preserved body of Vietnam's iconic leader. The remains are sent yearly to Russia, around October, for maintenance services. Security is strict and visitors are required to dress appropriately. People wearing shorts, miniskirts, and sleeveless dress/t-shirt are not permitted to enter. Visitors have to deposit their bags and cameras before they can be allowed to get in.

Operating Hours:
8AM to 11:00 AM   Tuesday to Thursday, and weekends
Close: Monday and Friday
Admission: Free
Address: At Ba Dinh Square in Hanoi city centre
Phone: +84 (4) 845 5128

Ho Chi Minh Museum

Ho Chi Minh museum is a memorial to the life of Ho Chi Minh and showcases mementos, war documents, rare pictures, artifacts and miniatures. You can hire an English-speaking guide for about 100,000 VND to help you navigate the extensive collections. Taking pictures is not allowed.

Visitors to the site often take a detour to a local market across where you can have a taste of local delicacies like Pho, the famous Vietnamese noodles, Che (pudding), baguettes, and other Vietnamese fares at much lower prices than their versions in the Old Quarter. It's also a good chance to mingle with the locals.

Address: 19 Ngoc Ha, Ba Dinh, Ha Noi
Operating hours: 8:00-11:30 AM, 2:00-4:30 PM

Open daily except Mondays and Fridays
Entrance fee: 10,000 VND
Website: www.baotanghochiminh.vn

Museum Of Vietnam History (bao Tang Lich Su)

The construction of this museum was completed by the Ecole Francaise d'Extreme-Orient in 1932 and it was originally called Louis Finot Museum. After the Vietnamese Government's takeover, the museum was opened for public viewing on September 3, 1958 under its present official name of Museum of Vietnam History.

The two-story museum offers a good overview of Vietnam's history in chronological sequence starting from the prehistoric times to the reading of the Declaration of Independence by President Ho Chi Minh. The 2,000 sq. m. building is a storage of thousands of precious objects of different origins attesting to the cultural diversity of Vietnam. Most items on display are labeled in Vietnamese.

The museum is located at the back of Hanoi Opera House.

Ticket Price: 20,000 VND, additional 15,000 VND for using your camera
Address: No.1 Pham Ngu Lao Street, Hoan Kiem District

Hoa Lo Prison

The Hoa Lo Prison was built by the French from 1886 to 1901 to hold Vietnamese prisoners. Then named Maison Centrale, the prison was used as a site for the torture and execution of political prisoners who were fighting for independence. During the Vietnam War, it was used by North Vietnam to confine prisoners of war. Among those who were imprisoned were Sen. John McCain whose flight suit still hangs as part of the display. Most of the exhibits focused on the sufferings of Vietnamese prisoners with no trace of the gory details that US POWs would later share in their memoirs and depicted in films like Hanoi Hilton.

Ticket:	30,000 VND
Address:	Hoả Lò, Trần Hưng Đạo, Hoàn Kiếm, Hà Nội, Vietnam
Phone:	+84 4 3824 6358

Vietnam Women's Museum

Vietnam Women's Museum is an exhibit of documentations about Vietnamese women's role in history and society, artifacts, and fashion. On display are women's fashion and jewelries through the years.

Ticket:	30,000 VND
Hours:	8:00AM to 5:00PM
Address:	36 Lý Thường Kiệt, Hang Bai ward, Hoàn Kiếm, Hà Nội, Vietnam
Phone:	+84 4 3825 9129

Thang Long Water Puppet Theatre

The famous Thang Long Water Puppet show traces its roots to the 11th century tradition that began in the Red River delta. Performances usually involve short sketches of village and agricultural life in the ancient times performed in a stage with a pool of water. Puppetters hidden behind the bamboo screen control the movements of the puppet. Accompanying live music makes the show more entertaining.

Hours:	daily, 3:30pm, 5pm, 6:30pm, 8pm and 9:15pm With 9:30am show on Sundays
Tickets:	40,000-60,000 VND
Address:	57b Đinh Tiên Hoàng, Hoàn Kiếm, Hà Nội, Vietnam
Phone:	(84-04) 3 824 9494
Fax:	(84-04) 3 824 5117
Email:	thanglongwpt@fpt.vn
Website:	www.thanglongwaterpuppet.org

Cúc Phương National Park

Cuc Phuon National park is Vietnam's oldest national park and nature reserve. It is located about 100 kilometer from the south of Hanoi and covers over 200 square kilometers of tropical forest and grottoes. The park houses the Endangered Primate Center with about 150 primates. Near the center is the Turtle Conservation Center, which you can explore for free. The park comes alive with butterflies during April and May. Bikes and motorcycles are available for rental.

Tickets:	park entrance, 20,000 VND The Endangered Primate Rescue Centre, 30,000 VND
Address:	Cuc Phuong, Nho Quan, Ninh Binh
Phone:	+84-3 03848 006
Fax:	+84-3 03848 052
Email:	dulichcucphuong@hn.vnn.vn
Website:	www.cucphuongtourism.com

Vietnam Museum of Ethnology

On display at this museum are artifacts, tribal arts and models of native houses. A nation with about 54 ethnic minorities, the museum highlights the many facets of Vietnam's multi-ethnic culture. Visitors are introduced to traditional activities like calligraphy and water puppet show. It is a worthwhile alternative to actually go to all remote places where Vietnam's minorities are located.

The museum is about 7 kilometers from the city center. A taxi ride will normally cost 200,000 VND. Alternatively, you can take the local bus no. 14, which leaves from P Dinh Tien Hoang and alight at the Nghia Tan bus stop. From there, you can walk to the D Nguyen Van Huyen which is about 600 meters away. Bus fare is 4000 VND.

Entrance:	25,000 VND
Hours :	8:30AM – 5:30PM Tuesday to Sunday
Address:	Nguyễn Văn Huyên, Nghĩa Đô, Cầu Giấy, Hà Nội, Vietnam
Phone:	+84 4 3756 2192

Nightlife in Hanoi

After the sun sinks below the horizon, Hanoi comes to life in a blaze of color and vibrancy. The energy of this enigmatic city can be felt throughout the city, with a variety of glittering nightclubs around the Old Quarter. This part is where you can find loud music, affordable drinks and socialize with locals. The city's strict laws mean that most clubs and bars will tend to close after midnight, but you'll discover quite a few won't actually turn away customers until the authorities arrive on the scene. Discover some of the best places to visit in Hanoi after dark.

Minh's Jazz Club

Minh's Jazz Club, located in Hanoi's French Quarter, is the most famous jazz club in the city. If you're after a place that plays the best jazz music, then definitely pay a visit. It opened back in 1998 by Quyen Van Minh, a Vietnamese jazz musician, who has performed in various countries worldwide. Minh's Jazz Club exudes a fantastically warm and atmospheric ambience, with dim yet warm lighting, great service and an even better drinks menu that features cocktails, beers, whiskeys, hot and soft drinks and a variety of Western and local bar foods.

Address: 1 Trang Tien Street, French Quarter, Hoan Kiem District, Hanoi

Funky Buddha Club

Located in Hanoi's French Quarter, the Funky Buddha Club is well-known for playing heavy bass and frequented by tourists, ex-pats, backpackers and the occasional Vietnamese local. The bar is spread out over two levels and plays house music until the authorities tell them it's time to close up. If you want loud music and cheap drinks, then the Funky Buddha Club is definitely the place for you.

Address: 2 Ta Hien, Hoan Kiem, Hanoi 100000

Halong Bay
Halong Bay is the most popular tourist destination in Vietnam. This magnificent spot of scattered islands, grottoes, caves and limestone karsts was recognized as a World Heritage site and it is undoubtedly Vietnam's most beautiful site. Most visitors prefer joining cruise tours around the bay as this is the easiest to arrange. You can also reach the Bay by taking a boat from the Bai Chay beach. The peak season is from May to August. Foggy weather from January to March reduces visibility but adds to the ethereal beauty of the site. You may want to consider visiting in November when the sky is clear and the crowd is thinner.

Location: Quảng Ninh Province

Chapter 13 – The Mekong Delta

The Mekong Delta is a huge network of swamplands, innumerable rivers, canals and islands where boats are the main modes of transportation. A comprehensive tour of the Delta allows visitors to observe and experience the way of life of people living in the area. A package tour is the cheaper and more convenient way to explore the delta but travelling independently is possible if you have more time and if you're willing to spend more.

My Tho

My Tho is the most accessible town in the Mekong Delta and a popular destination among tour groups. Tourists get to experience boat rides in long canals, visit factories making coconut candies, and enjoy fresh seafood. If you're travelling independently, you can take a bus at Ho Chi Minh's Cho Lon bus station for a two-hour ride to My Tho. Once you're there, you can charter your own boat and wander around.

The stunning area of My Tho is usually experienced by leaning back in a little boat as it cruises up a narrow canal, with palm trees lining each side of the bank. The main excursions here have long been a variety of traditional little food producers, such as honey farmers or coconut treats, before heading off to garden markets, a charming pagoda and then onto a café overlooking the restaurant.

Many of the trips to the My Tho area are usually done as part of a package trip based out of Ho Chi Minh City instead of My Tho itself. Visitors are herded onto buses and boats in order to keep the costs down, but you tend to be lost within a crowd.

However, if you head to My Tho yourself independently, you can organize your own trip. Several boat tour operators work around the river front. Prices may start around 400,000 dong but prices can – and will – drop to half this amount. However, the top tips here are to agree a complete price, itinerary and time-frame with each other before setting in the boat and NOT to hand over any money until you return. If accompanied by a guide, ask if their services are included in the initial fee or not. Again, do this before you get in the boat.

The beauty of the river is exceptional. With the sun gleaming down through the fringes of the palm trees, the lush greenery of the Mekong Delta really emphasizes how amazing it is here. When you get back on land, My Tho is a normal provincial town in Vietnam. Perhaps the most interesting areas of the town can be found along the side of the Bao Dinh River which runs perpendicular to the Mekong Delta. Unfortunately, not many colonial or traditional Vietnamese architecture has survived, but for a nice, shady area to rest from the intense heat of the sun, try going between Trung Trac and the Chuong Duong Hotel where there are numerous restaurants and cafes where you can relax with a cold drink.

Another attraction here is to slowly cruise from My Tho to Tan Chau, situated close to the border with Cambodia. It takes roughly a day and a half, sleeping on the boat, sometimes taking as long as three days. Boats are irregular and can be inquired about at the cargo pier.

Accommodation

Mekong My Tho Hotel

Located in My Tho is the superb Mekong My Tho Hotel. Offering fantastic service and accommodation for money, it is fast becoming one of the most popular hotels in the Tien Giang region. Situated around 28 miles from Vinh Long, the Mekong My Tho Hotel features an outdoor pool opening throughout the year, as well as a spa center, hot tubs, sauna, tennis courts, Wi-Fi, lounge area, gift shop, additional shops, free parking and a bicycle hire. Guests can choose from a range of garden, river or city view rooms, all with a flat screen television with cable; a number of rooms offer a seating area, ideal for relaxing in comfort. All rooms come with a private bathroom featuring a shower, free toiletries and slippers.

Address: 1A, Tet Mau Than, My Tho, Vietnam

Minh Kieu Hotel

The Minh Kieu Hotel is a charming two star accommodation in My Tho, situated around 37 miles away from Tan Son Nhat International Airport. It features a range of facilities and amenities, with light, airy rooms with air conditioning and a flat screen television with cable. A number of rooms boast a seating area, perfect for when you need to relax. All rooms comes with a private bathroom with free toiletries and slippers. With a good reputation for standards in service and accommodation, the Minh Kieu Hotel is certainly good value for money.

Address: 2 Thu Khoa Huan, My Tho, Vietnam

Ben Tre

Ben Tre is a smaller town, which is hardly visited by tourists. It's a two-hour bus ride from My Tho and there's little to catch the interest of travellers. Boat rides along the Delta canals are the main activities but if you're lucky, you'll have the entire boat to yourself.

Ben Tre Riverside Resort

Ben Tre offers a variety of good hotels, guesthouses and resorts, but the Ben Tre Riverside Resort certainly stands out from the other accommodation in the area. Located 26 miles from Vinh Long, it offers a variety of accommodation choices, a restaurant on site and boasts free parking and Wi-Fi.

You'll discover a variety of accommodation choices, some which feature separate seating areas for when you want to relax. Kettles are featured in all rooms, as are private en suite bathrooms, slippers flat screen televisions and a hairdryer.

The Ben Tre Riverside Resort offers complimentary shuttle buses to the Ben Tre Night Market, as well as free transport along the Ham Luong River if guests so wish. Other facilities at the hotel include a 24 hour front desk, a gift shop, bicycle hire and car hire. Since the area is popular with those who enjoy fishing, the hotel staff are a fountain of information for where the best spots are. The hotel is located 46 miles from the Tan son Nhat International Airport.

Address: 708 Nguyen Van Tu, Ben Tre, Vietnam

Mango Home Riverside

For those who like to travel green, the Mango Home Riverside is a beautiful environmentally friendly resort located within a verdant tropical garden in the heart of the Mekong Delta. It sits along the Ben Tre River, offering fresh and relaxing accommodation with Wi-Fi all throughout the resort. Guests can relax in the warm waters of the outside pool or soak up the sun on a sunbed. A verandah and lounge are two areas where guests can relax in solitude, with sunsets being particularly amazing from here.

All rooms at the Mango Home Riverside feature simple yet comfortable furniture, air conditioning, living area, wardrobes and fridges. Views overlooking the gardens make for a relaxing sight. The private bathrooms feature showers and free toiletries. All guests are welcomed with a gift of water, drinks and fruit in their rooms.

If you don't want to venture far in search for good food, then look no further than the on site restaurant. The hotel's garden supplies all the fresh and organic ingredients used in the beautifully prepared Vietnamese dishes served to guests. If guests are interested, they too can learn the art of cooking here at the Mango Riverside Hotel, in addition to the excursions and travel arrangements services. The front desk is served 24 hours a day and offers a range of services. Guests have the opportunity to make use of the free bicycles the hotel supplies to reach the local market. The Mango Riverside Hotel is situated nearly four miles from Ben Tre City.

Address: Nghia Huan Hamlet, My Thanh Village, Giong Trom, Ben Tre, Vietnam

Vinh Long
The Vinh Long is known for the Cai Be floating market but most people visit the town for its overnight accommodations to complete their Mekong Delta experience. Homestays can be arranged at the riverbank although the local tourist office

warns against the practice of dealing with unfamiliar operators.

Happy Family Guesthouse

The Happy Family Guesthouse is ideally situated just a short 12 minute walk away from the beach and close to the Mekong River. Featuring a range of simple yet comfortable cottages, all of which feature free Wi-Fi to use, the property is set within a lush garden full of green plants and a summing pool with sun terrace. The city of Vinh Long is located six miles away from the resort, Cai Be Floating Market a short thirty minutes away by boat and around a mile away from the Dong Phu Dunes.

The cottages available at the Happy Family Guesthouse are simply furnished yet tastefully decorated, with thatched roofs and wooden floors. Beds have mosquito nets to protect from the pesky little bugs, and a seating area gives you the perfect place to relax in. Guests do have to share bathroom facilities with showers, however. Other facilities at the Happy Family Guesthouse includes a laundry service, sun terrace, a lounge area and a travel desk to help with arranging excursions and onward travel arrangements. The restaurant located on-site features a range of tasty Vietnamese dishes to sample.

Address: 53/4 Phu My , Dong Phu, Long Ho, Vĩnh Long,

Phuong Thao Homestay

Located just over a mile away from the An Binh Ferry Stop, the Phuong Thao Homestay offers simple yet comfortable rooms for those looking for a cheaper accommodation option. The property is set in beautiful gardens, and offers a range of amenities and facilities at guests' leisure. Phuong Thao Homestay is situated around half a mile away from the Long Ho Relic.

Accommodation at the Phuong Thao Homestay is simple, with free Wi-Fi, mosquito beds to protect guests at night from the pesky little bugs, but bathrooms with showers are shared amongst guests. The restaurant at the property includes a variety of traditional southern Vietnamese dishes, some of which guests can learn how to cook for themselves at the hotel. Ideally situated, the Phuong Thao Homestay is a great choice for guests looking for basic yet comfortable accommodation suitable for those on a strict budget.

Address: An Thanh, An Binh, Long Ho, Vĩnh Long, Vietnam

Can Tho
Canto has a charming waterfront area, plenty of dining choices, and a great range of accommodations. Its floating markets are well-visited and you can reach them by sampan. Save on the fare by dealing directly with the paddler. The best floating market around is Cai Rang. You can negotiate with the paddler in the afternoon for a 5AM sampan ride to Cai Rang the following day.

Phu Quoc Island
Phu Quoc Island is home to exotic beaches and a great place for swimming and soaking in the sun. There are nearby fishing villages you can explore and plenty of food to feast on. To top it all, Phu Quoc Island is connected by flight to Ho Chi Minh.

Rach Gia
Rach Gia is located on the eastern fringes of the Gulf of Thailand around 270 kilometers from Ho Chi Minh City. It's a beautifully energetic port town, the capital of Kien Giang province. Referred to as the gateway to the Mekong Delta,

Rach Gia is usually visited by those passing through to Phu Quoc Island.

Rach Gia is also around 90 kilometers from Cambodia, so it's an excellent place to visit on your way to Kep. However, it's also a stopover point for those on the way to Nam Du, a scattering of 21 islands that aren't very well known to tourists. The islands are extremely beautiful, with verdant jungles, white sandy beaches, crystalline waters and an abundance of tasty seafood to enjoy. Only one ferry makes the journey each day but for those who love to explore the unknown, it's well worth it.

The majority of travelers who find themselves in Rach Gia will only really see the sights as they make their way from the ferry to the bus station (or the other way around). Once the sun sets, however, the city's energetic and vibrant side really comes out to play. After dark, the pathway to the bridge features a variety of different sellers, with many locals socializing on the bridge. On Ton Duc Thang Street, there are some excellent places to enjoy the sunsets, with various restaurants and cafes offering a variety of local dishes to enjoy.

Don't discount Rach Gia before you even reach here – there are some wonderful attractions to see. Pay a visit to Nguyen Trang Truc Temple on Nguyen Cong Tru. The temple is dedicated to the famous hero who stood up against the invading French colonists during the 19th century. The French tried numerous times to capture him but were never able to. In retaliation, the French captured his mother and several other locals and declared they would kill them if he didn't surrender immediately. He did so, and on the 27th October 1868 in the marketplace, they killed him.

The Kien Giang Museum is a little museum not visited much but it does features some interesting displays dating back to various time periods, such as skulls, pottery and jewelry dating between 100 – 600 CE. Other items showcased here include Khmer costumes, black and white photos from the war and other artefacts relating to Ho Chi Minh City. Outside the French colonial building where the museum is housed in is a US army helicopter wing where you can see bomb cases and a ten meter long whale skeleton.

From Rach Gia, the Superdong ferry takes the two hours and 20 minute journey to Phu Quoc three times a day. At weekends and during peak season, there are additional ferries which make the daily departures. The ferry is fast with assigned seats and air conditioning. During the rainy season – usually between May and June, there are only two departures to Phu Quoc each day. If the waters are too rough, then boats can be cancelled until the weather permits, so please bear this in mind when travelling here during the rainy time. If the water doesn't allow a boat trip to Phu Quoc, then there are flights which can get you there.

Sea Star Hotel
Located a thirty minute ride from Rach Soi Domestic Airport, and a short ten minute walk from Nguyen Trung Truc Temple, the Sea Stars Hotel is one of the best accommodation to stay in during your time at Rach Gia. Choose from a variety of different rooms, all featuring air conditioning, a working desk, a flat screen television with cable and fridge, the en suite bathrooms are well equipped with toiletries and a hairdryer. The restaurant at the Sea Stars Hotel provides a wonderful menu of Vietnamese cuisine, and other amenities on site includes free parking and Wi-Fi. The tour desk can help you

plan all your travel requirements, making it easy to get you to where you want to go.

Address: 2G5 Pham Hung Street, Rach Gia, Vietnam

The Palace Hotel
The Palace Hotel is ideally situated a sort ten minute walk from the Rach Gia Boat Station within the charming Hoa Bien area. Offering free parking and Wi-Fi throughout the property, it offers great service and value for money. With tiled floors, air conditioning, a working desk, flat screen televisions with cable, a fridge, living area and mini bar, rooms are light and airy. The en suite bathrooms includes showers and free toiletries.

The Palace Hotel is ideally located to the Rach Gia Bus Station and the local market, and offers luggage storage, ironing services and a travel desk to help with any excursions or onward travel arrangements. Guests can enjoy a delicious local-style breakfast in the lobby each morning at an extra charge and sample delectable delights at any number of the restaurants and cafes located within the vicinity.

Address: 20, Slot 12, 16ha Hoa Bien Area, Nguyen Hung Son, Rach Gia, Vietnam

Chapter 14 – Hoi An

Hoi An is an exquisite example of what a trading port city was like in Vietnam between the 15th and 19th centuries. Many historical buildings and monuments have survived, including the original layouts which incorporate a range of influences from both local and foreign cultures. The resulting mixture is a stunning town with at atmosphere not to be found anywhere else in the world.

There is no airport in Hoi An, and no train station either; the only way to get to and from Hoi An is via the road. It's a quick and easy taxi ride from close neighbor, Da Nang, where the local airport receives daily flights from Ho Chi Minh City, Hanoi and other major cities. Da Nang also boasts a train station which connects to other stations around the country, and there's always taxis cruising along the streets in the city, too.

Hoi An has a number of accommodation to choose from, including luxury hotels, guesthouses, hostels and homestays, with prices to reflect on whatever option you pick.

What To Do

My Son Sanctuary in Hoi An
The UNESCO World Heritage Site of My Son Hindu Sanctuary is the most popular attraction in Hoi An. For centuries, the ancient Champa civilization ruled the south of Vietnam, independent from the other cultures that flourished nearby between the second to 17th centuries. The Hindu influenced ruins are a spectacular mass of stone sculptures, towers, temples and other features amidst a lush jungle setting.

During it's time, My Son was the political and administrative center of the Champa civilization, as well as being the burial site for the royal family. There are over 70 buildings and monuments on the site which were dedicated to various Hindu deities, with the god Shiva being the most popular one, in addition to being considered the guardian of the Champa royal line.

The red-hued bricks and sandstone used in the construction of these monuments make the site stand out. Unfortunately, as with many historic sites, My Son has fallen to the ravages of time, abandoned by the people with nature covering her like a lush blanket. In 1898, the French attempted to restore it after it was accidently discovered; however, the war that soon followed meant that the Americans bombed the area. Since My Son was considered a sacred place, the Viet Cong believed that the Americans wouldn't cause any damage – a mistake that the site paid for. Thankfully, the majority of the complex managed to survive the devastation and archaeologists have managed to restore certain buildings and structures.

If you can't get to Cambodia and want to experience the grandeur and mystery of Southeast Asian cultures for yourself, then My Son is definitely well worth visiting. It's open all year through and is particularly amazing first thing in the morning before the rush of tourists.

Hoi An Old City
Between the 16th and 17th centuries, the coastal town of Hoi An flourished as one of the most influential and important trading towns. Trading with civilizations around Southeast Asia and beyond, today Hoi An is a perfect example of Eastern and Western influences when it comes to its architecture. As you

wander around the streets, you'll notice a mixture of Chinese temples, a Japanese style bridge, pagodas, timber shops, winding canals and colonial style residences. While other towns have given in to the pressures of progression, Hoi An has been able to preserve much of its historical buildings. As a result, wandering around Hoi An's Old Town can be somewhat likened to walking around a museum – the entire town is a showcase of her past. In December 1999, Hoi An's Old Town was proclaimed a UNESCO World Heritage Site.

At night, the beauty of the area is only enriched. Head to the riverside and marvel at the way the old fashioned lanterns illuminate the streets, creating a wonderful romantic area. Just a few kilometers away are two charming beaches for those who love to soak up the sun, but head back into town to try a fantastic selection of restaurants, get a suit handmade, meet the locals and simply bask in the warm, friendly atmosphere.

What makes Hoi An's Old Town incredibly nice is that you can easily explore it on foot and the traffic is minimal, especially when compared with other Vietnamese cities. A number of the streets only allow pedestrian's, bicycles and motorbikes – no cars allowed. Because of this, visitors are drawn here to experience Vietnam without the chaos and noise of city traffic. You'll see a mixture of architectural styles on the buildings in Hoi An's Old Town, many of which are over 100 years old, including Chinese styles, influenced by merchants from Guangzhou, Hainan, Fujian and other trading cities in China. As you pass by the shops, see if you can spot the business's name engraved and gilded with Chinese characters.

Japanese Covered Bridge
The Japanese Covered Bridge is perhaps one of the top five attractions in Hoi An. The Japanese bridge was constructed

back in the 18th century and is a stunning piece of Japanese planning. According to locals, it was erected by the Japanese who were living in Hoi An at the time so they could reach the Chinese part of town situated over the water. In 1719, Nguyen Phuc Chu Lord opened the bridge, engraving three Chinese characters across the top of the door in memory of the event.

Look closely and you will discover depictions of two dogs and two monkeys – these symbolize the year when it started (the year of the dog) and when it was completed (the year of the monkey), as well as symbolizing the Chinese years where numerous Japanese royals were born.

In 1986, the Japanese bridge began restoration, with the arch being restored after many years of it being flattened so that cars could pass through. Today, it stands testament to the beauty of the area, the influx of cultural influences at work throughout Hoi An's history and is just as beautiful as it was when it was first erected.

Head north of the bridge and you will come across a charming temple dedicated to Tran Vo Bac De, the Taoist god of weather. It's popular with locals who come here offering prayers in order to avoid any earthquakes. Standing guard along the bridges on both sides are statues of dog and monkeys. Look for the engraving of Chu Nho, which tells of all those who donated to the renovation work on the Japanese bridge. The Pagoda Bridge, also known as Cau Nhat Ban, links Tran Phu together with Nguyen Thi Minh Khai. Head over the bridge and you'll discover a treasure chest of art you can purchase, created by the various artists who live in the area. The bridge itself is 60 feet long, red and features a wooden roof. Due to its excellent conservation work, visitors can cross it any time of day as it's always open.

Accommodation in Hoi An

Villa Orchid Garden Riverside
The beautiful Villa Orchid Garden Riverside is ideally located within ten minutes drive of Hoi An's Old Town and the Quan Cong Temple. The hotel features an excellent restaurant featuring a range of delicious Vietnamese meals whilst guests relax with charming views over the garden. Cool off in the outdoor swimming pool or soak up the sun on the verandah before heading upstairs to the privacy of your room. Featuring air conditioning, deep baths to soak and flat screen televisions, the Villa Orchid Garden Restaurant offers great service and value for money.

Address: 32 Huyen Tran Cong Chua, Thanh Nam Hamlet, Hoi An
Phone: 0203 027 9779

Hoi An Garden Palace and Spa
The Hoi An Garden Palace and Spa is an award-winning hotel situated a short ten minute drive from the city's Old Town and Quan Cong Temple. Offering an airport shuttle 24 hours a day, guests can relax in the comfort of their light and airy accommodation before heading down to the restaurant within the complex, which offers a mouth-watering array of dishes. The Hoi An Garden Palace and Spa also offers guests the opportunity to pamper themselves at the spa center with a facial, a massage or any other treatments. Go for a dip in the outdoor swimming pool before relaxing with a drink in hand at the hotel's bar.

Address: 311 Cua Dai Street, Hoi An, Quang Nam
Phone: 0203 027 9779

Where To Eat

Visitors to Hoi An will discover an abundance of restaurants, cafes and other eateries throughout the city, some of the best within Hoi An's Old Town. Dine on a variety of dishes – both local and international – in the heart of the ancient district, where the soft lights of the old fashioned lanterns and the twinkling of the stars in the dark sky create a beautifully atmospheric background. The city is well-known for its excellent cuisine, especially it's white rose dumplings (or banh bao vac), and its chicken rice (com ga). You'll discover a variety of restaurants and cafes owned by ex-pats from all over the world where you can enjoy a few treats from home, including homemade ice cream, French desserts and many other delights.

Aubergine49 Restaurant

Aubergine49 is a wonderfully charming restaurant which serves a good selection of modern Eurasian dishes, homemade desserts and a fantastic array of wines. Vietnamese chef Nguyen Nhu Thinh has produced a beautiful variety of dishes with a unique twist, taking inspiration from his time in a three star Michelin restaurant in Tokyo, along with other international restaurants. You'll find delights such as roasted lamb, stuffed squid and a pistachio crusted goat's cheese. The banoffee pie with brandy snaps are definitely worth making room with. Open from Monday to Saturday between 6pm and 10pm, Aubergine49 is certainly one of the best restaurants you could visit in Hoi An.

Address: 49A, Ly Thai To Street, Hoi An
Phone: +84 510 221 2190

Hoi An Nightlife

When the sun sets in Hoi An, visitors will discover a completely different side. Gone is the sleep little city where history can be felt wherever you go; instead, Hoi An's vibrant and energetic side comes out to play. When it comes to entertainment, Hoi An has it all – nightclubs, cocktail bars, bistros, pubs, lounges – the majority of which can be found within the Old Town and Riverside. With the lanterns lit, you may even see some traditional folk dances being performed by locals and candles being lit before floating along the Thu Bon River. The rest of the country have to abide by strict curfews when it comes to evening establishments, but Hoi An's curfew seems to be much more relaxed. Many of the bars and clubs will stay open until around 3am, perfect for those who like to enjoy themselves, literally, all night long with locals and other visitors. You'll find cheap beer aplenty, with a wide variety of music being played. Read on to discover some of the best spots in Hoi An after the sun goes down.

Before and Now Bar

Before and Now Bar has been a popular after-dark entertainment spot for a few years but it's popularity has started to decline a little. Even with this, it's still frequented by visitors and locals looking for a vibrant place to drink and socialize. You'll find this bar around a five minute walk from the Japanese Covered Bridge and is spread over two levels, boasting an open-air terrace featuring lots of green plants. Lending it an air of casual friendliness, the Before and Now Bar boasts four happy hours which are two hours long each time.

Address: 51 Le Loi Street, Hoi An
Phone: +84 510 391 0599

Café 96
You will find the charming Café 96 on the banks of the river. With the exposed brickwork and the slightly peeling paint, Café 96 has an old fashioned, rustic charm that draws people in. Visitors can enjoy cheap beer in an fantastically casual and relaxed atmosphere. Café 96 also serves a variety of light bites for those who get a little puckish as they work the way through the drinks selection.

Location: 96 Bach Dang Street
Phone: +84 0510 910 441

Chapter 15 – Ha Long Bay

Ha Long Bay in northern Vietnam is perhaps one of the best known places in the country. Close to the border with China, Ha Long Bay is around 1,500 square kilometers of beautiful landscapes, which includes 1,600 limestone islands. In 1994, it was declared a UNESCO World Heritage Site. For a long time before that, though, Ha Long Bay has been drawing tourists here like moths to a flame with its stunning scenery and rich flora and fauna. The scenery itself has featured in numerous movies, dramas and magazines.

Ha Long Bay does not have its own airport. The best way to reach the area is via a long distance bus or car from Hanoi, which is roughly 170 kilometers away. If you don't mind splashing the cash, then visitors can opt to take a helicopter from the city to Ha Long Bay, which takes roughly an hour.

What To Do

Cat Ba Island
Cat Ba Island is undoubtedly the number one tourist destination in Ha Long Bay. The island can be reach by all the tour operators in the area, taking you on the trip to an island full of bars, hotels, restaurants, etc. – while the locals still carry on fishing in the traditional way. Explore the simple yet stunning beauty of the area.

Dau Be Island
For those who love to swim and dive, make sure you pay a visit to Dau Be Island. Dive underneath the crystal clear waters and discover a vibrant underwater world where the coral gleams.

The three inland lakes feature a variety of caves, only reachable via a rowing boat when the tides are low.

Dau Go Island
The main attraction on Dau Go Island is its beautifully big, colorful cave which wows visitors with its range of interesting and awe-inspiring stalagmites and stalactites, many of which have formed up to 20 meters tall.

Hung Sung Sot Cave at Bo Hon Island
Located on Bon Hon Island – the same island where the Virgin Cave can be found – Hung Sung Sot Cave amazes visitors with its squarish outer chamber and a ceiling that's 30 meters tall. Head into the inner chamber and you'll see the formations within resemble an army being talked to by their general. With the water reflecting light all around the chamber, it's something truly spectacular.

Pelican Cave at Bo Hon Island
Also located on Bo Hon Island is the Pelican Cave, often visited by tourists who enjoy taking photos of the beautiful formations within.

Virgin Cave at Bo Hon Island
The Virgin Cave is perhaps one of the best known attractions within Ha Long Bay. The shrine inside is dedicated to a beautiful woman who killed herself after running away from the Mandarin she was forced to marry. Upon her death, her body transformed to stone. Another legend tells of how a beautiful woman ran away from the Mandarin she was forced to marry in order to settle her father's debts. Fishermen found her lifeless body and buried her within the cave, creating a shrine to honor her memory.

Where To Eat

As can be expected due to its location, Ha Long Bay's cuisine typically features an abundance of seafood. The fish, oysters and other sea delights served to you in restaurants are generally caught earlier that morning, taken straight from the boats to the restaurants before visitor's have even rolled out of bed. There are many great restaurants to be found in Ha Long Bay Town, also known as Bai Chay Town, many situated along the beach. You'll find many restaurants focusing on Vietnamese, Chinese and seafood, but in the last few years, there's been an influx of western dishes to be found.

Green Mango Restaurant
Located on Cat Bar Island, the Green Mango Restaurant is a highly popular choice for those looking for great cuisine and top service. Guests can choose from indoor or outdoor seating, with views across the harbor as they dine on a range of exquisite fusion cuisine, tasty desserts and a range of good drinks.

Address: D 1-4, Cat Ba Town, Cat Ba.
Phone: +84 31 3887 151

Where To Stay

Ha Long Bay offers a variety of accommodation choices, from luxury cruise ships to boutique hotels and basic hostels and home stays for the budget conscious. Whatever your budget, whatever your taste, there's something for everyone here.

Halong Plaza Hotel

The Halong Plaza Hotel can be found in an excellent location to Halong Bay, close to the center, featuring an array of amenities and facilities including a sauna, gym, outdoor swimming pool and a variety of rooms to choose from. Accommodation at the Halong Plaza Hotel are light, airy and tastefully decorated, boasting air conditioning, satellite televisions, tea and coffee makers, with some rooms offering a comfortable living area with views stretching across the sea. Downstairs, the Four Seasons Restaurants offers guests a variety of cuisines – Thai, Western, Vietnamese and Japanese – making sure that no one leaves the table unsatisfied. The Bamboo Bar is ideal for a pre-dinner or after dinner drink, also offering a number of snacks. 24 hour room service is always handy for those who crave something at all hours of the night.

Work up a sweat at the well-equipped gym or within the sauna before relaxing with a massage. The outdoor pool is ideal for keeping fit and cooling off. For those who need to communicate with the office, Hotel Halong Plaza offers a variety of business services. Certainly one of the best hotels within the city.

Address: 8 Ha Long Road, Bai Chay Beach, Ha Long, Vietnam

Novotel Ha Long Bay Hotel
The Novotel Ha Long Bay Hotel is situated a stone's throw away from the beach, with views of the stunning Ha Long Bay seen from many areas of the hotel. Guests here will enjoy a range of light, airy and comfortable rooms which come with many amenities and high-tech gadgets. In the evening, take in beautiful views of the sun setting over the horizon from the comfort of your private balcony.

Address: Ha Long Road, Bai Chay Ward, Quang Ninh Province, Ha Long.

Conclusion

Once again thank you for choosing *Lost Travelers*!

I hope this book was able to provide you with the best travel tips when visiting Vietnam.

And we hope you enjoy your travels.

> "Travel Brings Power and Love Back to Your Life"
> - Rumi

Finally, if you enjoyed this guide, then I'd like to ask you for a favor, would you be kind enough to leave a review for this book on Amazon? It'd be greatly appreciated!

- Simply search the keywords "Vietnam Travel Guide" on Amazon or go to our Author page "Lost Travelers" to review.

Please know that your satisfaction is important to us. If you were not happy with the book, please email us with the reason so we may serve you more accordingly next time.

- Email: Info@losttravelers.com

Thank you and good luck!

NOTES

NOTES

NOTES

NOTES

Preview Of 'Peru: The Ultimate Peru Travel Guide By A Traveler For A Traveler

Around 20,000 years ago when humans migrated across the Bering Strait, some nomadic hunters and gatherers landed in Peru. They came to the country roaming in loose-knit bands. The early inhabitants lived in caves. They hunted mastodons, saber-toothed tigers, giant sloths and other fearsome animals. The existence and lifestyle of the early inhabitants were found in cave paintings that depict hunting scenes discovered in Toquepala and Lauricocha.

In 4000 BC, the inhabitants began to domesticate guinea pigs, alpaca and llama. Others suggest that it may have started way back in 7000 BC. Around this time too, people have begun planting seeds. They no longer relied solely on hunting for food. The people learned simple horticultural methods to improve their crops.

Today, Peru's coastal strip is a desert. Back then however, it was wetter. As a matter of fact, there were small settlements here. People tilled the land and planted crops like corn, squash, cotton, quinoa, beans and potato. They also fished using bone hooks and nets. They lived on sea lions, seabird eggs, sea urchins and shellfish. The people twined cotton to make their clothing; later though, they learned to apply weaving techniques.
Trade occurred in the Amazon basin. Evidences of trade relations between the Amazon and Andean regions include cassava, sweet potatoes, rainforest bird feathers and coca leaf among others. Although metalwork and ceramics were yet to be discovered by people in this period, they did craft jewelry from shell and bone.

The inhabitants of the coastal area built simple dwellings from reeds and branches with stone lining. They also built structures meant for rituals and ceremonies. The most complex and unique perhaps were the Caral ruins built around

3000 BC. There were astronomical observatories as well. The ruins of the oldest one were discovered north of Lima.

People also settled in the highlands. Although little is known about how these people lived, the structures they built are considered to be the most developed from this period. The earliest ruins from the highland settlers were found near Huánuco.

Organized life in Peru did not occur until the 2500 BC. Early Peruvian civilization evolved in the next 1500 years. During these times, various organized cultures emerged like the Chavìn and the Sechìn. The Chavìn were responsible for stylized religious iconography. Their influence spread to the whole coastal region. The Sechìn on the other hand, may not have had many cultural achievements but they are equally memorable for their military hegemony.

The Chavìn and the Sechìn culture and influence eventually declined which paved the way for the development of other regional cultures like the Saliner and the Paracas. These cultures were responsible for technological and artistic advances. They came up with weaving techniques which were more sophisticated than that of their predecessors. They also learned to make kiln-fired ceramics. After the Paracas, the Nazca emerged. We know the Nazca today for leaving a visible legacy. That is the cryptic and immense Nazca Lines....TO BE CONTINUED!

Check out the rest of Peru: The Ultimate Peru Travel Guide on Amazon by simply searching it.

Check Out My Other Books

Below you'll find some of our other popular books that are on Amazon and Kindle as well. Simply search the titles below to check them out. Alternatively, you can visit our author page (Lost Travelers) on Amazon to see other work done by us.

- Vienna: The Ultimate Vienna Travel Guide By A Traveler For A Traveler
- Barcelona: The Ultimate Barcelona Travel Guide By A Traveler For A Traveler
- London: The Ultimate London Travel Guide By A Traveler For A Traveler
- Istanbul: The Ultimate Istanbul Travel Guide By A Traveler For A Traveler
- Vietnam: The Ultimate Vietnam Travel Guide By A Traveler For A Traveler
- Peru: The Ultimate Peru Travel Guide By A Traveler For A Traveler
- Australia: The Ultimate Australia Guide By A Traveler For A Traveler
- New Zealand: The Ultimate New Zealand Travel Guide By A Traveler For A Traveler
- Dublin: The Ultimate Dublin Travel Guide By A Traveler For A Traveler
- Thailand: The Ultimate Thailand Travel Guide By A Traveler For A Traveler
- Iceland: The Ultimate Iceland Travel Guide By A Traveler For A Traveler
- Santorini: The Ultimate Santorini Travel Guide By A Traveler For A Traveler

- Italy: The Ultimate Italy Travel Guide By A Traveler For A Traveler

You can simply search for these titles on the Amazon website to find them.

Manufactured by Amazon.ca
Bolton, ON